To the librarians of Incline Village,
with thanks for all their help,
Hilary Hattner

DATE DUE

	DEC 1 7 2002
SEP 0 3 1996	
	2003
SEP 2 4 1996	
NOV 1 2 1996	SEP 1 8 2003
	MAR 1 0 2006
DEC 1 2 1996	AUG 0 7 2009
MAR 8 1997	4/14 LC
AUG 3 2000	
FEB 2 7 2002	
MAR 2 0 2002	
SEP 2 2002	
OCT 1 9 2002	
OCT 2 6 2002	
NOV 0 8 2002	

MYSTICAL DELIGHTS

Hilary Huttner

A Frontline Book

A Frontline Book is an imprint of Frontline Systems, Inc.,
P. O. Box 4288, Incline Village, NV 89450.
Copyright ©1996 by Frontline Systems, Inc.
All rights reserved.
Copyrights of individual poems are listed in the Copyright
appendix, which constitutes a legal extension of this page.
Printed in the United States of America by Thomson-
Shore, Inc. on acid-free paper to library specifications.

Cataloging-in-Publication Data
Huttner, Hilary, 1951-
    Mystical Delights/ by Hilary Huttner
    230 p. 22 cm. Index.
    ISBN 0-9647057-9-6 1st ed. (cloth)
        1. Enlightenment (General). 2. Mysticism and poetry.
3. Mysticism and literature. 4. Spirituality in literature.
5. Religion and poetry. 6. Mysticism. 7. Consciousness –
Religious aspects. 8. Experience (Religion). 9. Meditation.
I. Title.
149.3–dc20   95-61718
                                                        CIP

~ To my dear husband Dan ~
whose love makes all things possible

MYSTICAL DELIGHTS
HILARY HUTTNER 1996

CONTENTS

1. Introduction   1

2. A Doorway to the Sublime   5

3. Meditation and Transcendence   20

4. The Danger of Ignorance   66

5. Awakening   88

6. Essence   120

7. Unity   148

8. Mystical Delights   178

Conclusion   219

Copyright Sources   221

Index of Titles   229

Index of Authors   231

1

INTRODUCTION

For someone who is interested in learning more about the inner life, about consciousness and mystical insight, the works of the poets are a great resource. The gift of the poets is that when they write about the outer world, we get a sense of the inner life, and when they write about the particular, we get a sense of the universal. To read their poems is to share their joy and peace, to discover extrasensory delights, to learn metaphysical secrets, to awaken to the possibilities of enlightenment, to fall in love with the divine, to swing from universality to the tender being of things here and now, and in the end to come to a larger understanding of yourself.

In this book, we explore the works of the world's great poets for their mystical content. We look at poems that tell how the poets felt, what they saw, and what they concluded about reality. Their poems bear evidence of a common core of mystical experience that is part of our literary heritage worldwide, from ancient times to the present. They are an inspiring testimony to experiences of higher consciousness and insights into the mystic oneness of the universe.

The poets tell what it is like to awaken into peak moments of enlightenment. Exhilarated with a feeling of rebirth and personal freedom, they rejoice in a wide-awake appreciation of life. Sensing the spiritual essence of the created world, they hear and see the divine glory. They embrace a new, cosmic identity and a unity with all things. Marveling at the harmony of life, they feel sympathy with all living beings. Glad to be alive, they see life for what it is and have a sense of humor about it. They are blessed with inspired creativity, intuition, and inner strength. These are the fruits of an enlightened life.

The beautiful writings collected for this volume as examples of the growth of enlightenment are truly gems, whose beauty is established in the literary world but whose mystic meaning has yet to be fathomed. To enhance your understanding of the mystic meanings of the poems, they are organized in this book according to common themes, with a commentary to introduce the themes and notes to explain the relevance of each poem.

In the past, when poets have written about mystical experiences, their work has been dismissed as mere imagination by an unmystical readership. What to the uninitiated seems fanciful is to the wise a truthful description of the mystical reality. The poets write with uncanny accuracy.

Poetry is the natural speech of mysticism. Because the imagery and tone of a poem can convey more than ordinary words can express, poetic language is used to describe what would otherwise be inexpressible. Through image and tone, a poem can allude to an abstract experience or evoke a feeling which captures the after-effect of a mystical moment, even though the moment itself may have been beyond words. Poets, who have gifts of language beyond the ordinary, can put into words what other people can feel but cannot express themselves. That is why we like this poem, *Chosen Site*, by the popular Japanese poet Shuntaro Tanikawa:

in going there
words stumble.
in surpassing words
a soul gasps.
yet before that soul
something like a faint light is seen.

in going there
a dream explodes.
in piercing dreams
darkness glows.
yet before the picture's darkness
something like a large hole is seen.

Many cultures have made use of poetry to express mystical insight and to expand the mind's capacity for higher consciousness. In classical China and Japan, poetry was the natural accompaniment of the meditative life. Monks wrote poems to celebrate their awakening into enlightenment, and among laymen the writing of poetry became a means to cultivate sensitivity to Buddha-nature. Throughout the ancient world, poetry was the natural mode of language for mystical and religious scripture. The Vedas, Bible, Buddhist sutras and Koran rely on verse. The mystical function of poetry survives today in native cultures where poetry, praise, prayer and prophecy are blended into one, and verses learned by heart preserve metaphysical wisdom. It is no accident that the Eskimo word for poetry derives from the word for soul.

In studying the close association between mysticism and poetry, Henri Bremond concluded that poets conceive the germ of a poem in a naturally mystical state of consciousness. He believed that poems stimulated the mind of their reader so that the reader was led into the same deep level of awareness from which the poems had sprung. This resonance of inner awareness is a theory which readers will need to test for themselves! At least it may be claimed that poetry nourishes the mystical sensibilities of the mind and that as a result the mind feels more satisfied.

Mystical poetry is a blend of universality and individuality. The universality is colored by the unique personality of each poet and the culture in which the poet lived.

Yet through these filters, a universal consciousness shines and brightens the universality which is in each of us.

2

A DOORWAY TO THE SUBLIME:
The Mystical Power of Poetry

The Mysticism of Poetry

"A poem is the very image of life expressed in its eternal truth," said the great English poet Shelley.[1] A poem is a revelation, revealing the gleam of consciousness that moved the poet to write. Casting aside the confusion of the world, a poem focuses our attention on the true nature of life and communicates an impression of its spirit.

Because poetry is a form of intimacy with the ultimate nature of life, poetry is a form of mysticism. Poetry has been called *"that intercommunication between the inner being of things and the inner being of the human Self which is a kind of divination"*.[2] The mystical intimacy comes to the poet through inspiration and to the reader through acknowledgment of the ultimate nature revealed in the poem. The ultimate may be as simple as Williams' plums, *"so sweet, so cold"*, as lofty as Keats' axiom *"beauty is truth, truth beauty"*, as horrific as Ginsberg's *"nightmare of Moloch"*, and as universal as Whitman's *"vast similitude"*.

Poetry is a way of knowledge. Both science and poetry can describe the world, down to the most minute particulars, but only poetry can stretch to its sublime value. William Blake touched the sublime in *Auguries of Innocence*:

---

1. Because this chapter contains many footnotes, they are listed at the end of the chapter.

5

To see a World in a grain of sand,
And a Heaven in a wild flower,
Hold infinity in the palm of your hand,
And Eternity in an hour...

Poetry is mystical language. Compared with ordinary language, a poem is more highly organized, more compact, more symbolic and, in its elegant economy of expression and harmony of sound, more beautiful. Plato called poetry *"coiled language"* because in a poem there are many layers of meaning, referring back one upon the other. The tools of poetry (such as imagery and sound) and the resonance of each thought with the other thoughts within the poem all bring forth associations in the reader's mind. Through mental association, poetry has the power to evoke meanings that are beyond the meanings of ordinary language, sublime meanings in which concrete images reveal abstract truths.

"Poetry reaches out and touches mystery in its overflowing fullness, and stammers what it can of that experience. It expresses, through symbols and metaphors, that which is structurally unattainable by rational investigation..."[3]

Poetic Consciousness

The language of a poem is evidence that it arises from a special mental state, in which communication is of a higher order than the poet's ordinary thinking or speech. In such a state, the poet perceives an expanded meaning, a fundamental nature and an importance in the images that come to mind. Snatches of memories of other moments of insight come together, related by a sense of the present moment. Creative associations bring disparate thoughts together in similes and metaphors, revealing what they have in common. The poet's language becomes so ingeniously organized that it surprises even the poet, as meaning and form arise together in rhythmic lines and repetitions of letters and rhymes come spontaneously. The sound of the words seems perfectly suited to their meaning, as though the phrases were animated by the same eternal truth they describe.

Where does this burst of greater creative intelligence come from? How is it that thoughts and language can arise spontaneously with such order and perfection? Many poets have explained the phenomenon of their own inspiration in terms of an Intelligence greater than their own.

True poets draw their inspiration from a profound depth, and it is the greatness of the level of being from which the inspiration is drawn that makes the poems great. The modern English poet and novelist D. H. Lawrence described the inspiration of a poem as *"life springing itself into utterance from its very wellhead."*[4] A century earlier in England, the poet Coleridge described inspiration as *"the infinite I AM reverberating in the Imagination."*[5]

Inspiration surged so strongly in the English poet William Blake that he felt his long poems were being dictated to him by divine will. In a letter to a friend in 1803, Blake wrote:

> *"I have written this Poem from immediate Dictation, twelve or sometimes twenty or thirty lines at a time, without Premeditation & even against my Will; the Time it has taken in writing was thus render'd Non Existent, and an immense Poem Exists which seems to be the Labour of a long Life, all produc'd without Labour or Study. I mention this to shew you what I think the Grand Reason of my being brought down here."*[6]

In America, the poet and essayist Ralph Waldo Emerson also sensed the transcendent origin of inspiration. In his essay *The Poet*, he made a claim so fantastic that it bears a second reading, especially because he expected that every intellectual person would be able to learn it:

"It is a secret which every intellectual man quickly learns, that beyond the energy of his possessed and conscious intellect, he is capable of a new energy (as of an intellect doubled on itself), by abandonment to the nature of things; that beside his privacy of power as an individual man, there is a great public power on which he can draw, by unlocking at all risks his human doors, and suffering the ethereal tides to roll and circulate through him; then he is caught up into the life of the Universe..."[7]

This is the greatness of inspired works, the greatness of the cosmic life of the universe. This life takes shape in the form of a poem when the poet abandons himself to the state of inspiration, when *"the ethereal tides [of the] great public power...circulate through him."*

For T. S. Eliot, inspiration was less sensational and more modern. Eliot found inspiration to be more like a flash of higher consciousness, a moment when the obstructions of stress and ignorance are remarkable by their absence and consciousness is freed to function in a new way. Eliot described inspiration as:

"the sudden lifting of the burden of anxiety and fear which presses upon our daily life so steadily that we are unaware of it . . . the breaking down of strong habitual barriers—which tend to re-form very quickly. Some obstruction is temporarily whisked away."[8]

Inspiration is a time of purity. However impure the poet may be at other times in his life, at the moment of inspiration, the ideal poet's mind becomes a pure reflection of the true nature of life. The more innocent the poet is at the time of inspiration, the more natural his poem will be. The innocent reflection of reality—how well it is captured in this anonymous poem, written long ago in eighth century China:

The wild geese fly across the long sky above.
Their image is reflected upon the chilly water below.
The geese do not mean to cast their image on the water;
Nor does the water mean to hold the image of the geese.[9]

To put poets in their place, it should be pointed out that all human beings have access to the same universal source of inspiration and creativity. But ordinary thoughts are like a dim view from a distance. They view life from a vantage point far removed from the ultimate source.

Inspired thoughts are like a view close-up. The view is close to the source of life because the inspired poet's awareness has temporarily expanded to a fundamental level. So the poet sees closely into the fundamental nature, and that enables him or her to describe it vividly.

When we read poetry, the poet's inspiration inspires us to dig down deep in our awareness to understand his or her communication on the level from which it came. Then we remember that this profound level had always been in us, only we had passed it by. We recognize the truth in the poets' descriptions, because somehow we had already seen what they are describing but had not consciously appreciated it.

The ultimate nature of life, the poet's intimate view which becomes the poem, the reader's profound response, all three find common ground in one wholeness of existence. Together they re-enact the eternal drama of consciousness knowing consciousness. In reading a poem, we draw closer to our own being.

The Reader's Consciousness

Poetry cultures the mind by expanding awareness. Stimulated by a poem, the mind goes beyond its ordinary thinking to appreciate the poem's unordinary language, its high degree of organization, its beauty, its imaginative associations, its insights. In appreciating that communication, the mind of the reader becomes like the mind of the poet at the time of inspiration. Going beyond ordinary thinking, the mind transcends from the unrelated and inconsequential to the universal and eternally true. Getting the gist of a poem is not merely a horizontal expansion of knowledge, like getting your facts straight. It is getting to a more profound level of consciousness where, says Shelley, *"A poet participates in the eternal, the infinite, and the one..."*[10]

As your mind moves in the direction of a more profound level, your intellect may not always follow. You may be left wondering why you like a poem, why it transports you as a beautiful piece of music transports you, why it has a significance that you cannot express. Without knowing why, you may feel a liberating joy as your awareness expands beyond its old boundaries. To the extent that reading poetry stimulates you to transcend, it is a mystical experience.

How poetry stimulates the mind to transcend has been brought to light by Dr. Rhoda Orme-Johnson in a comprehensive article, *"A Unified Field Theory of Literature"*. Transcendence may be triggered by meanings that take the mind inward to absorb them, by swinging the reader's attention from the concrete to the abstract, by descriptions of higher states of consciousness that remind readers of their own experiences, or by literary techniques such as figurative language, gaps, and rhythm. In a poem, the figurative language (in which one thing is associated with another) *"encourages the reader to transcend to a subtler, more intuitive, holistic level of consciousness in order to connect the disparate objects involved..."*[11] The *"gaps"* in the poem also encourage a shift in consciousness. The gaps may be gaps in meaning which the reader fills in, the juxtaposition of contrasting values, or the gaps may be moments of silence built into the form of the poem, as the gaps between the stanzas.

The silence is an important part of the structure and effect of the poem. In the pauses of the poem and in the special silence afterwards, the mind digests what it has read and has the "aha!" experience of insight.

Another major influence on the reader is rhythm. The rhythm of a poem arises from its accented syllables, its pattern of vowels, its phrases, and the arrangement of words on the page. Rhythm settles the mind and yet keeps it alert enough to have insights in that settled state. The rhythm communicates the flow of the poet's consciousness. It conveys an emotional tone and sometimes seems to capture the rhythm of life itself.

Inherent in the phrasing of a poem is a rhythmic breathing pattern that was there at the time the phrases and pauses were created and which re-emerges as the most appropriate breathing pattern when the poem is read. As the state of the body and mind are related, so too the rhythmic flow of breath and the flow of consciousness are related.

A vocal champion of the relationship between rhythm, breathing and consciousness is the contemporary American poet Allen Ginsberg. He explains:

"So you find in Blake or any good poetry a series of vowels which if you pronounce them in proper sequence with the breathing indicated by the punctuation ... you find a yogic breathing ... that ... will get you high physiologically. ... And so I think that's what happened to me in a way with Blake."[12]

What happened to Ginsberg with William Blake's mystical verses was an experience of higher consciousness. He was only twenty-two at the time, reading Blake's poetry in his apartment in New York. Ginsberg tells his story:

"I had my eye on the page, and I heard a big, solid, solemn earthen voice saying Ah, Sunflower, weary of time. My voice now, actually....reciting first The Sunflower, then The Sick Rose and then The Little Girl Lost....At the same time, there was outside the window a sense of extraordinarily clear light....Everyday light seemed like sunlight in eternity....And then I looked further at the clouds that were passing over, and they too seemed created by some hand to be conscious signals....I had the impression of the entire universe as poetry filled with light and intelligence and communication and signals....Kind of like the top of my head coming off, letting in the rest of the universe connected into my own brain....There was a sense of an Eternal Father completely conscious caring about me in whom I had just wakened. I had just wakened into his brain, or into his consciousness, a larger consciousness than my own. Which was identical with my own consciousness but which was also the consciousness of the entire universe. So basically it was a sensation of the entire universe being completely conscious."[13]

Don't rush off to read Blake's verses just to repeat Ginsberg's experience. It was a unique moment in the flow of Ginsberg's life. You will have the experiences that are the fruit of your own consciousness.

The value of reading poetry shows itself in a new appreciation of ordinary life. If a poetic mood lingers as you go about your day, you may find that the clouds seem majestic as the breath of God, the fruits at the market look like works of art, and the people waiting in line at the bank seem like characters in an endless story of evolution. Reading poetry encourages an intimate appreciation of the sublime suchness of things, and a feeling of unity with them.

Poetry has *"the power of so dealing with things as to awaken in us a wonderfully full, new and intimate sense of them and of our relations with them. When this sense is awakened in us, as to objects without us, we feel ourselves to be in contact with the essential nature of those objects, to be no longer bewildered and oppressed by them, but to have their secret and to be in harmony with them. This feeling calms and satisfies us as no other can. "*[14]

A reader may pick up a poetic state of mind from reading poetry because words have the power to convey the state of mind of their creator. The organization of the words reflects an organization of consciousness, a style of functioning which is appropriate for poetic thoughts. Picking up on that style, the reader finds himself or herself in a state of expansive thinking.

"To read the poets poetically—I do not say to understand them—is more or less to resemble them; it is to associate oneself with them, to share in their gift, in their poetic state. "[15]

Is it any surprise that reading poetry puts one in a poetic frame of mind? Anyone who has attended a poetry workshop knows how reading other people's work puts one in the mood to write one's own poems. There are stories of great poets who were so moved by reading the works of a fellow poet that they created a new poem in response. When Coleridge heard Wordsworth in person reciting his poem *Prelude*, Coleridge was inspired to write a poem *To William Wordsworth* to express the effect the *Prelude* had on him:

Scarce conscious, and yet conscious of its close
I sate, my being blended in one thought
(Thought was it? or aspiration? or resolve?)
Absorbed, yet hanging still upon the sound—
And when I rose, I found myself in prayer." [16]

Coleridge raised an interesting point, which was echoed by Henri Bremond (author of *Prayer and Poetry*) and A. Allen Brockington (author of *Poetry and Mysticism on a Basis of Experience*): For Coleridge, a minister's youngest son, the effect of an inspiring poem was akin to the mysticism of private prayer.

The great American poet Longfellow noticed a similar benediction. He wrote in praise of poetry in his poem *The Day is Done*:

Such songs have the power to quiet
The restless pulse of care,
And come like the benediction
That follows after prayer.

Like the perfection of grace, the perfection of poetry is soothing. Poetry is a refuge from chaos. *"The sense of wholeness, of everything coming together, of resolution— is one of the primary pleasures of poetry."* [17] Its orderliness smoothes out knots of stress and quiets *"the restless pulse of care,"* replacing unease with a meditative state of quiet breathing, joy and healthful wholeness. How beautifully Keats put it in his poem *Endymion*, which begins:

A thing of beauty is a joy forever:
It loveliness increases; it will never
Pass into nothingness; but still will keep
A bower quiet for us, and a sleep
Full of sweet dreams, and health, and
*   quiet breathing.*

We have described the poetic state of mind and body that the reader gains from contact with poetry, but of course there is more—the meaning of the poems and their mystical insights. *"Nothing more disgusts the serious artist than to be praised for his manner and neglected for his content."*[18] The wisdom of poetry should not be ignored, clash though it may with the conventional world view, because to ignore its mystic meaning is to ignore our own higher nature. Like the best of teachers, the poems communicate both knowledge and a heartfelt appreciation of that knowledge. This is the kind of wisdom which becomes a part of you—*"felt knowing"*.[19]

If you have had mystical experiences, you will find the poems in this book helpful in putting into words some of what you have experienced and in valuing that experience. Many of the poems are about the first glimmerings of higher consciousness. The insights in the poems and the commentary that accompanies them will round out your own understanding. The knowledge will, as the poet Keats promised, *"ease the Burden of the Mystery."*[20]

If you have not yet had mystical experiences, you may discover a new dimension within yourself because poetry exercises the mystical sensibilities of the mind. The mind stretches to accommodate the mental stimulation of poetry as naturally as the eye expands and contracts to accommodate visual stimulation. As with any human ability, stimulation encourages it to flower, and a lack of stimulation leads to atrophy or denial. For higher thought, we need higher food for thought.

If you are familiar with mystical experiences, the poems will make sense. But if you are new to such thought, the poems may, at first, seem unrealistic or obscure. It often happens with mystical works that if you already understand the experience or insight, the writing is an obvious statement of the way things are, but if you don't have a prior understanding, then the writing seems to have an unimportant or fanciful meaning. In this book, the introduction to each chapter and the notes to the poems are meant to level the playing field for all readers by giving them the esoteric background to understand at least one interpretation of the poems. Use the commentary as a springboard for your own understanding.

The real test of poetry is how it affects *you*. You may find, as Walt Whitman suggested, that *"The greatest poet brings the spirit of...events and passions and scenes and persons...to bear on your individual character."*[21] In this book are samples of poems by Whitman and many other poets for your experimentation. Imbibe them in small doses, let them do their work; then verify their effect in the great laboratory of your own life.

It does not matter if the language of poetry is new to you. The more you read poetry, the more you will grow into it. Some poems are meant to be read several times until the whole poem falls into place like a puzzle. Most of the poems in this book are short, easy to read and suited to modern tastes.

Many pleasures await you in this volume: wondrous experiences, mind-expanding images, the perfect marriage of sound and meaning, humor, tenderness and haunting beauty. Yet most stirring are the moments of heartfelt truth captured in the poems. It is the heartfelt truth that compels the poet to write and the reader to read.

FOOTNOTES

1. Percy Bysshe Shelley, *A Defense of Poetry,* ed. Albert Cook (Boston: Ginn & Co., 1903), p. 10.

2. Jacques Maritain, *Creative Intuition in Art and Poetry* (Cleveland: The World Publishing Company, 1953), p. 3.

3. Elizabeth Wilhelmsen, *Cognition and Communication in John of the Cross* (New York: Peter Lang, 1985), p. 130. Quoting Robert Herrera's comment on the poetry of St. John of the Cross.

4. Ekbert Faas, *Towards a New American Poetics* (Santa Barbara, California: Black Sparrow Press, 1979) p. 12. Quoting A. Beal, *Selected Literary Criticism* (New York: Viking, 1956), p. 167.

5. Ibid., p. 167. Quoting Samuel Taylor Coleridge, *Biographia Literaria*, ed. G. Watson (London: Dent, 1965), p. 87.

6. A. Allen Brockington, *Mysticism and Poetry On a Basis of Experience* (Port Washington, N.Y.: Kennikat, 1970) p. 85-86.

7. Ralph Waldo Emerson, "The Poet," in *Essays* (Boston: Houghton Mifflin, 1883), p. 80.

8. T. S. Eliot, *The Use of Poetry and the Use of Criticism* (Cambridge: Harvard University Press, 1933), p. 137.

9. Chang Chung-yuan, *Creativity and Taoism* (New York: Harper Colophon, 1963), p. 57.

10. Percy Bysshe Shelley, *A Defense of Poetry,* ed. Albert Cook (Boston: Ginn & Co., 1903), p. 6.

11. Rhoda F. Orme-Johnson, "A Unified Field Theory of Literature," *Modern Science and Vedic Science*, 1:3 (1987), p. 356.

12. Paul Portuges, *The Visionary Poetics of Allen Ginsberg* (Santa Barbara, California: Ross-Erikson, 1978), p. 79.

13. Anne Waldman and Marilyn Webb, *Talking Poetics from Naropa Institute*, Volume Two (Boulder: Shambhala, 1978), pp. 383-395. Quoting poet Allen Ginsberg.

14. Henri Bremond, *Prayer and Poetry,* trans. Algar Thorold (Burns Oates & Washburne, 1927), p. 64.

15. Ibid., p. 3.

16. A. Allen Brockington, *Mysticism and Poetry On a Basis of Experience* (Port Washington, N.Y.: Kennikat, 1970), p. 130.

17. Donald Hall, *The Pleasures of Poetry* (New York: Harper & Row, 1971), p. 6.

18. Ananda Coomaraswamy, "The Normal View of Art," in *The Christian and Oriental Philosophy of Art*, ed. Ananda Coomaraswamy (New York: Dover, 1956), p. 33.

19. Philip Dow, *Nineteen New American Poets of the Golden Gate* (New York: Harcourt Brace Jovanovich, 1984), p. 7. Quoting poet Jack Gilbert.

20. Anne Waldman and Marilyn Webb, *Talking Poetics from Naropa Institute* (Boulder: Shambhala, 1978), p. 23. Quoting a letter written by Keats on May 3, 1818.

21. Walt Whitman, "Preface," in *Walt Whitman*, ed. Mark Van Doren (New York: Viking, 1945), p. 39.

List of Poems in Chapter Three

Lines, Composed a Few Miles above Tintern Abbey
by William Wordsworth

The Infinite
by Giacomo Leopardi

The Holy Longing
by Johann Wolfgang von Goethe

Stanzas Concerning an Ecstasy
by San Juan de la Cruz

Chosen Site
by Shuntaro Tanikawa

Tea at the Palaz of Hoon
by Wallace Stevens

A Song
by Richard Crashaw

The Curative Powers of Silence
Al Young

Song of the Prophet to the San Juan River
Traditional Navaho

Prayer
by George Herbert

If Only There Were Stillness
by Rainer Maria Rilke

Gitanjali (CIII)
by Rabindranath Tagore

Shores of Silence
by Karol Wojtyla, Pope John Paul II

3

MEDITATION AND TRANSCENDENCE

Whether by nature or intention, there are times when the mind and body slip the boundaries of ordinary wakefulness and enter into an expanded state of awareness, a meditative state. This state is both mental and physical, so that an adjustment of either the mind or the body will bring about a constellation of effects which involves the whole person. It is a style of functioning which is more quiet and more broad-based than ordinary waking, as the ocean bed is more quiet and more broad-based than the surface waves. It is a more fundamental and more universal level of existence. When the body and mind of the small, individual self are quieted, the unbounded Self is revealed. This revelation makes the meditative state a cornerstone of mysticism and higher consciousness.

The physiological state of meditation is easy to identify. It can be measured in a laboratory. The neurophysiological findings show that oxygen consumption and pulse rate diminish, while brain waves change to a coherent pattern emanating from both lobes of the brain.[1] The scientific findings are much like the account given by Wordsworth in his poem *Lines, Composed a Few Miles above Tintern Abbey*:

> *. . . that serene and blessed mood,*
> *In which the affections gently lead us on,—*
> *Until, the breath of this corporeal frame*
> *And even the motion of our human blood*

1. Robert Keith Wallace, "The Physiological Effects of Transcendental Meditation," in *Scientific Research on the Transcendental Meditation Program Volume I*, ed. David Orme-Johnson and John T. Farrow, (Livingston Manor, N. Y.: M.E.R.U. Press, 1977), pp. 48-52, 60-65.

Almost suspended, we are laid asleep
In body, and become a living soul:
While with an eye made quiet by the power
Of harmony, and the deep power of joy,
We see into the life of things.

Meditation begins with ordinary wakefulness. Added to this familiar mode of thought is an expansion of one's awareness to quieter levels, where subtler forms of perception and thought, even no thought, are possible. This quiet awareness comes naturally when the body becomes quiet. This is the inner peace of meditation. It is a state of restful alertness. The Italian poet Leopardi described the unboundedness and inner peace of meditation in his poem *The Infinite*:

My thought discovers vaster space beyond,
Supernal silence and unfathomed peace;
Almost I am afraid; then, since I hear
The murmur of the wind among the leaves,
I match that infinite calm unto this sound
And with my mind embrace eternity . . .

When inner peace is taken to its most fundamental level, something happens which is difficult to describe, transcendence. To transcend means to go beyond. In going beyond, a junction is crossed between the sphere of life bounded by time, space and the activity of change, and the realm which is eternal, unbounded and unchanging. It is the junction between the individual and the universal, between the small self and the unbounded Self. When transcendence occurs, individual life is temporarily suspended in cosmic life.

In transcending, even a talented poet like Shuntaro Tanikawa admits, *"Words stumble."* Words stumble because in going there, one has left ordinary words behind.

One has taken leave of ordinary thoughts and ordinary sensations as one turns one's attention inward. One is on the brink of a new experience, for which the old descriptions of the world do not suffice.

What happens? At first, it is not obvious. Goethe said curtly, *"You are gone."* Yet he recognized that this is a way *"to grow"*.

As one becomes familiar with the process of transcending in a meditative state, one develops the flexibility to experience it and remember it, too. A long description of transcendental awareness can be found in the poem *Stanzas Concerning an Ecstasy Experienced in High Contemplation* by the mystical Spanish poet San Juan de la Cruz, who called transcendence a state of *"unknowing"*:

He who truly arrives there
Cuts free from himself;
All that he knew before
Now seems worthless,
And his knowledge so soars
That he is left in unknowing
Transcending all knowledge.

As the mind follows the inward stroke of meditation through the subtler strata of awareness, there may arise unusual and delightful experiences, such as the inner *"light"* Shuntaro Tanikawa saw. Many poems describe experiences of higher consciousness and divine perception. In *Tea at the Palaz of Hoon*, Wallace Stevens describes the perception of a spiritual substance and sacred vibrations:

Out of my mind the golden ointment rained,
And my ears made the blowing hymns they heard.

Stevens goes on to say, *"I was myself the compass of that sea: I was the world in which I walked."* The experience of meditation is the experience of the inner self, which is both individual and cosmic. From the cosmic perspective, everything is united within one Self and is an expression of that Self.

To expand to the universality of transcendental consciousness, the mind must let go its mundane individuality and the body must cease its usual activity. This temporary cessation, especially noticeable in the breathing pattern, has led some writers to describe the meditative state as a kind of death, although in the positive sense of a purifying transition to a new, higher life. In his devotional poem *Song*, the metaphysical poet Richard Crashaw described the suspension of individual life in cosmic life when he wrote the line *"Dead to my selfe, I live in Thee."* He pursued this theme in the following lines:

Though still I dy, I live again;
Still longing so to be still slain,
So gainfull is such lose of breath.

Body, mind and soul find rest in meditation. This rest has a practical value in daily life because it alleviates the impact of worldly stress. The soothing effect of the meditative state is apparent in a tranquil poem, *"The Curative Powers of Silence"* by Al Young. In a state of awareness so pure it is *"wordless"*, he is able to let *"the pre-mind dream/ of nothing at all"* and then finds himself in a state of surrender *"not even dreaming/—being dreamed"*. The tranquility of meditation is like the Navaho river of *"broad water. . . flowing water. . . ancient water"*.

The meditative state, with its peace, bliss and appreciation of the infinite, is sometimes considered by religious writers to be a form of prayer. George Herbert's poem *Prayer* is an accurate description of a good experience in meditation. He describes the nature of prayer as:

Softnesse, and peace, and joy, and love, and blisse. . .

The inner peace of meditation is conducive to contemplation of the divine because it is a time when one lets go of the distractions of the outer world and turns one's attention inwards to the transcendent silence. From ordinary silence one progresses to the *"supernal silence"*, described so well by Leopardi. *"If only there were stillness, full, complete"* Rilke sighed to God, *"Then in a thousandfold thought I could think you out..."* Since ancient times, the wise have taught the value of inner silence, as does this prayer to the Egyptian god Thot:[2]

O Thot, you are a sweet well . . .
When the silent man approaches, the well
    reveals itself;
When the noisy man comes, you remain hidden.

In the quiet, expanded awareness of the meditative state, the religious person finds an advantage. There subtle perception of the divine seems possible. There one may drink from the well. In that rapport, the devotee's offering of prayer, love and one's very self seems unobstructed. The Indian poet Rabindranath Tagore knew this advantage. He wrote: *"In one salutation to thee, my God, let all my senses spread out and touch this world at thy feet. . . . let all my mind bend down at thy door."*

This chapter on meditation, peace and transcendence ends with the age-old distinction between the mystical, meditative states and religious states. It is the distinction between oneness and twoness. The bliss of meditation is an unbounded oneness, in which individual life becomes cosmic life. The bliss of religion is a loving duality

---

2. Excerpted from *Prayer to the God Thot*, translated by Ulli Beier, as found in Alan Lomax and Raoul Abdul, eds. *3000 Years of Black Poetry* (New York: Dutton, 1970), p. 28.

between two participants, the devotee and the divinity. Thus the subtle contrast between the mystical poem of Leopardi, whose mind embraces eternity, and the devotional poem of Pope John Paul II, who has an embrace within eternity with *"Someone from beyond"*. Yet both experiences have the same point of departure. Pope John Paul II writes in his poem *Shores of Silence*:

> *The distant shores of silence begin*
> *at the door. You cannot fly there*
> *like a bird. You must stop, look deeper,*
> *still deeper, until nothing deflects the soul*
> *from the deepmost deep.*

*   *   *

Next follows the text of the poems described in this essay, in the order in which they were discussed. The accompanying notes explain their mystical relevance. This format of introductory essay, poems and notes will be used for all of the remaining chapters.

Most of the poems presented in this book are short, sparkling gems. The next selection, however, is a long poem typical of Wordsworth, from which we have excerpted the most beautiful and most quotable passages. Wherever verses have been skipped, we have followed the convention of printing asterisks to mark the omission.

WILLIAM WORDSWORTH
(England, 1770-1850)

LINES, COMPOSED A FEW MILES ABOVE TINTERN ABBEY

Five years have past; five summers, with the length
Of five long winters! and again I hear
These waters, rolling from their mountain-springs
With a sweet inland murmur. Once again
Do I behold these steep and lofty cliffs,
That on a wild secluded scene impress
Thoughts of more deep seclusion; and connect
The landscape with the quiet of the sky.

*   *   *

These beauteous forms,
Through a long absence, have not been to me
As is a landscape to a blind man's eye:
But oft, in lonely rooms, and 'mid the din
Of towns and cities, I have owed to them,
In hours of weariness, sensations sweet,
Felt in the blood, and felt along the heart;
And passing even into my purer mind,
With tranquil restoration:—feelings too
Of unremembered pleasure: such, perhaps,
As have no slight or trivial influence
On that best portion of a good man's life,
His little, nameless, unremembered acts
Of kindness and of love. Nor less, I trust,

To them I may have owed another gift,
Of aspect more sublime; that blessed mood,
In which the burthen of the mystery,
In which the heavy and the weary weight
Of all this unintelligible world,
Is lightened:—that serene and blessed mood,
In which the affections gently lead us on,—
Until, the breath of this corporeal frame
And even the motion of our human blood
Almost suspended, we are laid asleep
In body, and become a living soul:
While with an eye made quiet by the power
Of harmony, and the deep power of joy,
We see into the life of things.

                    *   *   *

                    And I have felt
A presence that disturbs me with the joy
Of elevated thoughts; a sense sublime
Of something far more deeply interfused,
Whose dwelling is the light of setting suns,
And the blue sky, and in the mind of man:
A motion and a spirit, that impels
All thinking things, all objects of all thought,
And rolls through all things. Therefore am I still
A lover of the meadows and the woods,
And mountains; and of all that we behold
From this green earth; of all the mighty world
Of eye and ear,—both what they half create,
And what perceive; well pleased to recognise
In nature and the language of the sense,
The anchor of my purest thoughts, the nurse,
The guide, the guardian of my heart, and soul
Of all my moral being.

*   *   *

                    And this prayer I make,
Knowing that Nature never did betray
The heart that loved her; 't is her privilege,
Through all the years of this our life, to lead
From joy to joy: for she can so inform
The mind that is within us, so impress
With quietness and beauty, and so feed
With lofty thoughts, that neither evil tongues,
Rash judgments, nor the sneers of selfish men,
Nor greetings where no kindness is, nor all
The dreary intercourse of daily life,
Shall e'er prevail against us, or disturb
Our cheerful faith, that all we behold
Is full of blessings. Therefore let the moon
Shine on thee in thy solitary walk;
And let the misty mountain-winds be free
To blow against thee.

*   *   *

Notes

The original title of this poem is *Lines*, and below that
is the note *"Composed a few miles above Tintern Abbey, on
revisiting the banks of the Wye during a tour. July 13,
1798."* Hence the common name for this poem, *Tintern
Abbey.* The poem, however, is not about an abbey but
about the higher consciousness that Wordsworth felt in the
presence of nature. This theme is most clearly expressed
in the four passages that we have excerpted from the original, which is 158 lines long.

Wordsworth gives us clues in his other writings, such
as his poem *Intimations of Immortality from Recollections
of Early Childhood*, that he had perceptions of divine glory
as a child and rapture as a youth rambling through the
woods but lost those experiences later in life. Wordsworth
felt hampered by the fretful stir of cities. In this poem, he
returns in his maturity to the countryside where he is
inspired with *"a sense sublime"*. He also writes that he has
"oft" had such experiences, even *"'mid the din of towns"*,
when he recalls the effect of Nature on him.

The woodland scene that opens the poem is a description of the natural world. Yet this description also has parallels with an inner state of mind. As the poem progresses,
this mental state, engendered by Nature, becomes the
theme of the poem. The *"sweet inland murmur"*, the *"lofty
cliffs"*, the *"deep seclusion"* and the *"quiet of the sky"* all
lead to an inward mental state of quietude and joy, a
meditative state which Wordsworth calls *"that serene and
blessed mood"*.

Wordsworth's description of the *"blessed mood"* is a
classic description of a meditative state. He begins with
one of the most noticeable boons of meditation, that *"the
heavy and the weary weight/ Of all this unintelligible
world,/ Is lightened"*. Although Wordsworth does not

elaborate, typically such lightening takes places on three levels: There is a physical sense of lightness in the body; there is a psychological relief from the stress of *"the dreary intercourse of daily life"* (described in the final excerpt), and there is a spiritual liberation from ignorance (*"the burthen of the mystery"*) and from the chaos of the *"unintelligible world"*. In all these ways, the activity of the world does not make as heavy an impression as it did before.

Wordsworth says that his *"affections"* play a role in leading him on into *"that serene and blessed mood"*. This observation is in keeping with the reports of countless mystics who refer to the heart, the heart center, the heart's desire, devotion and a deep appreciation of the divine as forces that draw one into meditation. Wordsworth is drawn by an affection for Nature, arising from his deep appreciation of the sublime spirit pervading Nature.

Corresponding to his mental state of quietude is a physical state of deep rest. In the deep rest of a meditative state, metabolism decreases, reducing the need for the heart and lungs to work. The pulse rate and the volume and frequency of breath decrease. Wordsworth experienced this dramatically. He observed that *"the breath of this corporeal frame/ And even the motion of our human blood/ Almost suspended, we are laid asleep/ In body"*. This *"asleep in body"* is not ordinary sleep. It is only like sleep in that it is a state of rest. Wordsworth remains alert. He has spontaneously fallen into the state of restful alertness which is characteristic of meditation.

When the activity of the body is *"laid asleep"*, Wordsworth becomes aware of being *"a living soul"*. Certainly he was a living soul all along, but it is when the distraction of the body is suspended in the quietude of his meditative state that he becomes aware of the more subtle feeling of his own soul.

Not only does he sense his own soul; he also sees *"into the life of things."* This expanded perception follows when the *"eye"* and the consciousness that governs perception are made *"quiet"* (that is meditative) by the power of *"harmony"*. In the meditative harmony, there is a state of calm, orderliness and attunement that is both individual and cosmic. When the mind and body settle into a meditative state, they become more orderly. Being more orderly, Wordsworth is drawn closer to his true nature. Being closer to his true nature, he is attuned to the true nature of all things and sees *"into the life of things"*.

Another important element of Wordsworth's state is *"the deep power of joy"*. Joy, rapture, ecstasy, bliss, happiness, love—these become more than feelings in the state of meditation; they are the essential mode of being. They are the individual's reflection of the divine or metaphysical bliss of existence. This reflection is mirrored in Wordsworth's poem. His joy is both part of his own inner state and akin to the presence that he sees in Nature, so that just to look on Nature disturbs him with *"the joy of elevated thoughts"* and stimulates him with the excitement of bliss.

When Wordsworth looks on Nature, he sees *"a presence...deeply interfused"*. Not only does he see this presence in Nature, he also senses it in the human mind. Finding one common presence in Nature and in *"the mind of man"*, and indeed in *"all things"*, Wordsworth unites the objective, outer world and the inner, subjective mind in one spiritual basis. He has hit upon a central perception of mysticism, the universal Soul:

A motion and a spirit, that impels
All thinking things, all objects of all thought,
And rolls through all things.

In all modesty, he credits Nature with engendering in him the *"joy...quietness...beauty... [and] lofty thoughts"* of his victorious insight and for giving him a *"cheerful faith"* that can withstand the pettiness of daily life. Nature is his spiritual retreat and his inspiration, the dwelling place of his own higher nature.

GIACOMO LEOPARDI
(Italy, 1798-1837)

THE INFINITE

I always loved this solitary hill,
This hedge as well, which takes so large a share
Of the far-flung horizon from my view;
But seated here, in contemplation lost,
My thought discovers vaster space beyond,
Supernal silence and unfathomed peace;
Almost I am afraid; then, since I hear
The murmur of the wind among the leaves,
I match that infinite calm unto this sound
And with my mind embrace eternity,
The vivid, speaking present and dead past;
In such immensity my spirit drowns,
And sweet to me is shipwreck in this sea.

Translated by Lorna de' Lucchi

Notes

The Infinite describes a classic experience of meditation. In solitude, the poet is *"lost"* in contemplation. Losing is the easiest way to slip into a meditative state because no effort is required to lose oneself, to surrender. This art is formalized in meditative techniques, such as the losing and losing of T'ai Chi and Transcendental Meditation.

Having lost the limits of the mundane world, quickly the poet transcends to a state of unboundedness, the *"vaster space beyond"*. There he finds *"supernal silence"* and *"infinite calm"*.

Unbounded, beyond space and time, the poet's mind expands to *"embrace eternity"*. In such expansion, the poet cannot maintain the experience of his own individuality, and so he *"drowns"*. This drowning is a blissful merging, like a drop merging with the ocean to enjoy its greater depths, *"and sweet to me is shipwreck in this sea."*

JOHANN WOLFGANG VON GOETHE
(Germany, 1749-1832)

THE HOLY LONGING

Tell a wise person, or else keep silent,
because the massman will mock it right away.
I praise what is truly alive,
what longs to be burned to death.

In the calm water of the love-nights,
where you were begotten, where you have begotten,
a strange feeling comes over you
when you see the silent candle burning.

Now you are no longer caught
in the obsession with darkness,
and a desire for higher love-making
sweeps you upward.

Distance does not make you falter,
now, arriving in magic, flying,
and, finally, insane for the light,
you are the butterfly and you are gone.

And so long as you haven't experienced
this: to die and so to grow,
you are only a troubled guest
on the dark earth.

Translated by Robert Bly

Notes

"The holy longing" is a longing for transcendence. Transcendence is a time-out, when individual life is suspended in cosmic life. Goethe calls their union *"a higher love-making."* It is also, in a metaphorical sense, a *"death"* because it is a cessation and a radical change in the usual experience of the individual self's existence. One's usual experience is a state of ignorance of the divine light. Goethe calls that state *"an obsession with darkness."* Yet, through an intense desire for the *"light"*, one may escape being *"caught"* and instead be swept *"upwards."* That upward sweep is like *"magic"* because it is beyond the usual reality. Because a flying butterfly magically metamorphosizes from a creeping caterpillar, the *"butterfly"* represents a transformation to our highest self, which is attracted to the divine light as a moth is to a candle flame.

What happens when you arrive, when you transcend? Goethe simply says, *"You are gone."* That is how it is described at the end of the Buddhist Heart Sutra: *"Gone, gone, gone beyond, altogether gone beyond."*[3] You go beyond the senses, beyond words, to a state of absolute being, and it is when you come out of it that you understand what has happened and you feel the bliss of that *"higher love-making"*. This bliss is the missing balm for fulfillment. *"And so long as you haven't experienced this...you are only a troubled guest on the dark earth."*

---

3. Anonymous translation, *The Heart Sutra* (Cambridge, Mass.: Cambridge Zen Center, 1989), p. 4.

STANZAS CONCERNING AN ECSTASY
EXPERIENCED IN HIGH CONTEMPLATION

I entered into unknowing,
And there I remained unknowing,
Transcending all knowledge.

I entered into unknowing,
Yet when I saw myself there
Without knowing where I was
I understood great things;
I shall not say what I felt,
For I remained in unknowing
Transcending all knowledge.

That perfect knowledge
Was of peace and holiness
Held at no remove
In profound solitude;
It was something so secret
That I was left stammering,
Transcending all knowledge.

I was so whelmed,
So absorbed and withdrawn,
That my senses were left
Deprived of all their sensing,
And my spirit was given
An understanding while not understanding,
Transcending all knowledge.

He who truly arrives there
Cuts free from himself;

---

4. Born Juan Yepes y Alvarez, he is also known as St. John of the
Cross.

All that he knew before
Now seems worthless,
And his knowledge so soars
That he is left in unknowing
Transcending all knowledge.

The higher he ascends,
The less he understands,
Because the cloud is dark
Which lit up the night;
Whoever knows this
Remains always in unknowing
Transcending all knowledge.

This knowledge in unknowing
Is so overwhelming
That wise men disputing
Can never overthrow it,
For their knowledge does not reach
To the understanding of not-understanding,
Transcending all knowledge.

And this supreme knowledge
Is so exalted
That no power of man or learning
Can grasp it;
He who masters himself
Will, with knowledge in unknowing,
Always be transcending.

And if you should want to hear:
This highest knowledge lies
In the loftiest sense
Of the essence of God;
This is a work of His mercy,
To leave one without understanding,
Transcending all knowledge.

Translated by K. Kavanaugh and O. Rodrigues

Notes

Transcending is usually beyond words, but San Juan de la Cruz describes it with such familiarity that meditators from very different traditions can recognize in his *Stanzas* a description of the universal experience of mystical transcendence.

What San Juan de la Cruz calls *"high contemplation"* we call meditation. His *"ecstasy"* has four attributes: enrapt attention, understanding beyond conception, *"the union of the soul with God"*[5] and spiritual bliss. What he calls discursive and imaginative meditation,[6] which he advises is only for beginners, is meditating on something (such as Christ crucified) for the sake of inspiration rather than for the state that transcends concepts.

When ordinary thought, and hence ordinary knowledge, are transcended, a state of abstract, pure awareness obtains. In this poem, it is called the state of *"unknowing"* and *"transcending all knowledge"* because it is unlike the conventional way of knowledge of the *"wise men disputing"*. Although the discrimination of the outer world is left behind, the abstract nature of existence remains. The attributes of this abstract, spiritual existence are the *"great things"* which are *"understood"* by intuition. Thus in the state of transcendence, there can arise a paradoxical experience when the intuition takes on a consciousness of great metaphysical truth and yet the ordinary thinking process is in a state of suspension, of unknowing. This is the experience of *"an understanding while not understanding"*.

The attributes of *"peace"* and *"holiness"* and *"solitude"* are experienced intimately in meditation. *"That*

---

5. St. John of the Cross, *Ascent of Mount Carmel*, trans. and ed. E. Allison Peers (Garden City, New York: Doubleday, 1958), p. 357.
6. Ibid., p. 128.

perfect knowledge" does not come by way of intellectual learning but by participating in the esoteric *"secret"* or hidden nature of *"the essence of God"*. The ecstasy of this participation is so absorbing (*"I was so whelmed"*), that the attention naturally turns inward towards this bliss, and the senses easily forego their outer *"sensing"*.

"He who truly arrives there/ Cuts free from himself." When the senses cease sensing, one loses awareness of one's body and environment, and when the mind is *"absorbed"*, one loses concern for one's individual self. When the mind is no longer gripped by one's own individuality, one is liberated from the constraints of that individuality. Thus from body, mind and selfhood, one *"cuts free"* in meditation.

In cutting free, there is an expansion in which intuitive, metaphysical *"knowledge so soars"* that all previous consciousness of more limited things seems *"worthless"* in comparison. This idea could also be expressed as 'consciousness so expands'.

The cryptic lines *"The less he understands/ Because the cloud is dark"* do not indicate ignorance but rather the transcendent nature of *"something so secret"*. The *"less he understands"* indicates a different state of mind than ordinary understanding, different because it turns away from the multiplicity of the world to *"less"* of the world and more of the God beyond human conception. Though words such as *"dark"* and *"cloud"* may be used by other writers to indicate spiritual obscurity, San Juan de la Cruz gives these words his own meanings, which probably are based on his contemplative experience in his dark cell. He assigns three meanings to the *"dark"* and the *"night"*: 1) deprivation of the senses and worldly desires, 2) faith (because it leads beyond where the understanding can see), and 3) God (because He cannot be seen nor fully conceptualized).[7] The image of the cloud may refer to a mass of awareness, which may be colorless or white. Perhaps it is akin to this Taoist experience of deep meditation:

As soon as one is quiet, the light of the eyes begins to blaze up, so that everything before one becomes quite bright as if one were in a cloud.[8]

Such mystical knowledge is sorely missing from the knowledge of the *"wise men disputing"*. Historically, the dispute between San Juan de la Cruz and the Catholic faction who opposed him was not about mysticism but about the asceticism of his reforms. His opponents kidnapped and imprisoned him. At night, in the quiet and concealment of darkness, he journeyed in contemplation and began to compose poems which he recited after his escape. Thinking of him there, one can well imagine how the cloud of unknowing at night would be infinitely preferable to the harsh reality of his days.

The *Stanzas* continue:

He who masters himself
Will, with knowledge in unknowing,
Always be transcending.

The promise that mastery of the self will lead to the transcendental state is much like the promise of the spiritual practices of India and Asia. There are techniques to transcend the limitations of the surface level of one's individual life and appreciate the divine life which transcends it. In time, familiarity with transcending leads to the coexistence of transcendental awareness with ordinary consciousness, enlightening that consciousness.

---

7. St. John of the Cross, *Ascent of Mount Carmel*, trans. and ed. E. Allison Peers (Garden City, New York: Doubleday, 1958), p. 22.
8. Richard Wilhelm and C. G. Jung, *The Secret of the Golden Flower* (New York: Harcourt, Brace & World, 1967), p. 50.

The poem concludes by identifying the *"highest knowledge"* with *"the essence of God"*. That state of knowledge in unknowing, *"that perfect knowledge . . . of peace and holiness"* is a state of pure knowledge and of pure being. It is both knowledge about the divine essence and the spiritual state of that essence. Transcending to that state, one gains an experiential knowledge of the essence. This, says San Juan de la Cruz, is *"a work of His mercy"*.

SHUNTARO TANIKAWA
(Japan, 1931-)

CHOSEN SITE

in going there
words stumble.
in surpassing words
a soul gasps.
yet before that soul
something like a faint light is seen.
in going there
a dream explodes.
in piercing dreams
darkness glows.
yet before the picture's darkness
something like a large hole is seen.

Translated by Harold Wright[9]

Notes

Shuntaro Tanikawa is one of Japan's most popular contemporary poets. His sensitive descriptions of everyday life and meditative experiences are bound to make him a favorite in the United States, too. This poem is about experiences that occur when the eyes are closed in a state of deep silence. It is a description of a mind stretching to apprehend subtle levels of being.

9. Oriental poetry is sometimes translated without punctuation marks. We have taken the liberty of adding punctuation to Mr. Wright's fine translation for readers who need this aid.

The *"chosen site"* is a plane of transcendence within the mind. In going there, the mind settles down to a more abstract, unbounded, quieter, less overtly pronounced way of thought. The usual mental stream of words becomes vaguely pronounced in the mind and may even disappear. Also, as the mind goes beyond its usual experience, words become inadequate to describe the experience. These may be the reasons that the poet writes, *"words stumble."*

The phrase *"a soul gasps"* suggests awe in the transcending experience of *"surpassing words"*. It conveys the kind of awe that takes the breath away. When the mind goes into a meditative state, the body also goes into a meditative state and metabolizes less and breathes less. After a period of reduced breathing, the lungs will fill with a gasp, indicating that the body is coming out of an episode of deep rest or transcendence. This experience would come after *"a soul gasps"* because the body's gasp is an outer sign that there was an inner state of suspension.

The use of the word *"soul"* is a good sign, a sign of consciousness awake enough to be aware of its soul. Because the poet does not define the soul, it is sufficient to understand it here as a fundamental level of his being.

Aware, at that fundamental level of being, the poet has a vision with his eyes closed. In his mind, *"something like a faint light is seen."* This is a classic experience encountered by people in meditative and religious states. In a state of inner quiet, when one's mind settles down to an awareness of one's own thought at the most fundamental level from which it first manifests, at that fundamental level, one can sometimes appreciate the first manifestation of creation, which appears to the human nervous system as light. On a metaphysical level, this *"light"* is the first vibration of creation. On an individual level, it is the liveliness of the soul's consciousness. On a universal level, it is the glow of the glory of the divine life of creation.

The experience of light is described more fully in this passage by the medieval German mystic Hildegarde of Bingen:[10]

> *Since my childhood, I have always seen a light in my soul, but not with the outer eyes, nor through the thoughts of my heart; neither do the five outer senses take part in this vision. . . . The light I perceive is not of a local kind, but is much brighter than the cloud which bears the sun. I cannot distinguish height, breadth or length in it. . . . What I see or learn in such a vision stays long in my memory. I see, hear, and know in the same moment. . . . I cannot recognize any sort of form in this light, although I sometimes see in it another light that is known to me as the living light. . . . While I am enjoying the spectacle of this light, all sadness and sorrow vanish from my memory.*

There is also another, less esoteric explanation for the light. The alternative explanation is that when the human body shuts down, it sees light as an artifact of the process of shutting down. Both in death and in meditation, the body reduces its physiological activity (far more so in death) and indeed, in near-death experiences and sometimes in meditation, light and a tunnel are seen.

The subject of a tunnel brings us to the next stanza of the poem, which concludes with a vision of a large hole. The second stanza has a structure parallel to the first. However, whereas the first stanza focused on light and the affirmation of something there, the second stanza focuses on the yin of darkness and the void of a hole.

The second stanza begins, *"in going there/ a dream explodes."*[11] As in Japanese monks' poems of awakening,

---

10. Richard Wilhelm and C. G. Jung, *The Secret of the Golden Flower* (New York: Harcourt, Brace & World, 1967), p. 106.
11. The translator chose to run the stanzas together.

the dream refers to the old mental reality, a state of ignorance and delusion.

The poem continues, *"in piercing dreams/ darkness glows."* The piercing of the dream, a variation of the mystic metaphor of piercing or parting the veil of delusion, is an indication of surpassing the old state of mind, as was *"surpassing words"* in the first stanza.

"darkness glows" is an experience of the enlivenment of the darkness. It does not refer to light because the stanza emphasizes the *"picture's darkness"*, which is not a metaphorical darkness (not ignorance) but something seen as in a picture in the mind's eye. When the impulses of thought are reduced in a meditative state, the background emptiness becomes a palpable darkness. The sense of enlivenment in that void is a sense of the liveliness of sheer, absolute being. This experience does not involve light because it is a sense of the potentiality of the uncreated. Yet a poet might use the phrase *"darkness glows"* as the most economical way to describe the liveliness of the void.

The poem concludes, *"something like a large hole is seen."* People who transcend in meditation sometimes connect transcendence with the sensation of slipping down a hole into a state of unknowing. They also associate the image of a hole opening up with a clearing in the mass of their awareness. Having gone from the subtle level of the manifested glory (the faint light described in the first stanza) to the subtler level of the lively potentiality of the void, (the darkness described in the second stanza), there lies ahead through the large, fathomless hole the possibility of an unknown realm of even more absolute existence.

WALLACE STEVENS
(United States, 1879-1955)

TEA AT THE PALAZ OF HOON

Not less because in purple I descended
The western day through what you called
The loneliest air, not less was I myself.

What was the ointment sprinkled on my beard?
What were the hymns that buzzed beside my ears?
What was the sea whose tide swept through me
    there?

Out of my mind the golden ointment rained,
And my ears made the blowing hymns they heard.
I was myself the compass of that sea:

I was the world in which I walked, and what I saw
Or heard or felt came not but from myself;
And there I found myself more truly and more
    strange.

Notes

Wallace Stevens is one of the great poets of twentieth century America. He is a master of the right word and the just so phrase. He describes with subtlety the inner experience of a person toying with the first glimmers of higher consciousness. His shorter poems which we have selected for this book have a readable, cool mystique. Yet the sophisticated vocabulary, upper-class tone and abstruseness which characterize some of his other poems have kept Stevens from "pop" popularity in the New Age. His works have been misinterpreted as philosophical speculations rather than as realistic descriptions of a person wrestling with the dilemma of dawning enlightenment, the dilemma of a person who sees the world sometimes with higher and sometimes with lower consciousness and who has to reconcile the two realities himself, without any help from the doctrines of his culture.

Tea at the Palaz of Hoon is one of Stevens' early poems of mystical experiences. In the first line, he asks us not to think less of those experiences because they have the quality he associates with *"purple"*, the qualities of twilight and imagination. He advises us, *"not less was I myself."* Indeed, he comes to the conclusion in the last line, *"there I found myself more truly"*. He descends into the depths of his mind, as the sun descends below the horizon. His journey is as lonely as *"the loneliest air"* because it is a journey of the self alone.

Stevens reports two flashy experiences: hymns and a golden ointment. Stevens recognizes that they are inner experiences but does not explain their significance. The only explanation we know of comes from the tradition of Yoga, where these experiences are known as celestial perception. They are subtle sensations of the inner senses, not illusions, but perceptions of the finest level of life.

Traditionally, the buzzing hymns are said to be the fundamental vibrations which are the precedent to material form. Traditionally, the golden substance is the most refined substance which mediates between the immaterial and the material and enables bliss-consciousness to be expressed in the body. Occasionally it floods out when one is in a meditative state and gives the mind the impression of golden drops or sweet drops. This nectar-like substance is also considered to be a key part of a change in the style of functioning of the mind and body, a change to a higher state of consciousness. Indeed, the next experience Stevens reports is a new, higher state of consciousness.

Stevens' journey of self-discovery leads to an experience of unity, that time-honored consciousness in which the individual and the universe are experienced as one Self. Stevens concludes, *"I was the world in which I walked"*. This is not an ego-trip; this is the ego changing perspective from the small self to the big Self, which is the great, all-encompassing Reality.

Tea at the Palaz of Hoon was published at the same time as another poem by Stevens, *The Snow Man*. *Tea at the Palaz of Hoon* has a Yogic flavor, which is expressed in the inner-sensory experiences and the unity consciousness, reminiscent of the 'I am so' self-realization of Yoga. *The Snow Man* has a Zen flavor, which is expressed in its description of the *"mind of winter"* and the metaphysical emptiness, reminiscent of the 'just so' realization of Zen. *The Snow Man* concludes:

> *For the listener, who listens in the snow,*
> *And, nothing himself, beholds*
> *Nothing that is not there and the nothing that is.*

Stevens was influenced by reading Oriental poetry and other books which gave him a survey of Asian and Indian philosophy. He read Okakura's *Ideals of the East.*[12] He wrote in a letter, *"...it soothes me to think that I'm reading the latest Japanese authors."*[13] He also admired the Oriental treatment of landscape in poetry, painting and gardens. In his library notes, he wrote, *"Landscape-Gardening—another art of Chinese origin aimed at a definite influence on the beholder's mind."*[14] That aim is to culture a Zen-like state of mind in the garden's visitors. Stevens' understanding of that art shaped the mind of the beholder in *The Snow Man.*

Later in his life, Stevens wrote more personal descriptions of his own awareness of reality, an awareness which caused Stevens some self-doubt as he evolved from the old state of consciousness to the new. Towards the end of his life, he described an enlightening *"elevation"* in his poem *"As You Leave the Room"*:

And yet nothing has been changed except what is
Unreal, as if nothing had been changed at all.

---

12. Joan Richardson, *Wallace Stevens, the Early Years* (New York: Beech Tree Books, William Morrow, Inc., 1986), p. 246.
13. Ibid., p. 341.
14. Holly Stevens, *Souvenirs and Prophecies* (New York: Knopf, 1977), p. 221.

RICHARD CRASHAW
(England, 1612-1649)

A SONG

Lord, when the sense of thy sweet grace
Sends up my soul to seek thy face,
Thy blessed eyes breed such desire,
I dy in love's delicious Fire.

O love, I am thy sacrifice.
Be still triumphant, blessed eyes.
Still shine on me, fair suns! that I
Still may behold, though still I dy.

Though still I dy, I live again;
Still longing so to be still slain,
So gainfull is such lose of breath.
I dy even in desire of death.

Still live in me this loving strife
Of living Death and dying Life.
For while thou sweetly slayest me
Dead to my selfe, I live in Thee.

Notes

This poem employs a metaphor for transcending that crops up a variety of cultures. It is the metaphor of dying. Yet this is not an ordinary death, it is the temporary end of the limitations of the individual self, so that the person may experience a more exalted life, to *"live in Thee"*.

Laboratory measurements of modern meditators who transcend have shown that, around the time of transcendence, the breath is suspended. Loss of breath may have reminded earlier writers of the idea of dying. Crashaw's reference to *"such lose of breath"* is an indication that he experienced the physical suspension of transcendence.

Why brave such a death? Because it is blissful, and because one does not really die, one just steps out of time into eternity. Crashaw tells us *"So gainfull is such lose of breath"* because it is *"delicious fire"* that *"sweetly slayest me"* and *"Dead to my selfe, I live in Thee."*

When Crashaw says *"Thee"*, he speaks of a divine Lord that is separate from himself. Yet he unites with the Lord in love so closely that he finds *"I live in Thee."*

Crashaw falls into a meditative state through a combination of grace and religious passion. His desire turns his mind in the right direction, but it is grace which *"sends up my soul"*.

AL YOUNG
(United States, 1939-)

THE CURATIVE POWERS OF SILENCE

Suddenly
I touch upon wordlessness,
I who watch Cheryl
the blind girl who lives up the street
walking at night
when she thinks no one's looking
deliberately heading into hedges & trees
in order to hug them
& to be kissed,
thus are we each
hugged & kissed,

Wordless
I fill up
listening for nothing
nothing at all

as when in so-called life
I am set shivering with warmth
by a vision
with the eyes closed
of the Cheryl in me
when I think no one's looking,
plopped down in a field of grass
under watchful trees

letting the pre-mind dream
of nothing at all
nothing at all

no flicker
no shadow
no voice
no cry,

not even dreaming

—being dreamed

Notes

"Suddenly/ I touch upon wordlessness," the poet tells us. He is entering a mode of silent appreciation that is beyond words. He is appreciative of the blind girl's closeness to the trees she cannot see. He, too, feels close to the trees and the grass, close even to the essential nothingness surrounding them, as he listens, Zen-like, *"for nothing at all"*.

He knows how to enter a meditative state, how to rest in a more quiet, more fundamental mode of the mind, *"letting the pre-mind dream/ of nothing at all"*. His mind attains a yogic stillness, with *"no flicker"*, like the ancient Indian lamp in a windless place. In this state, he is not doing anything; Nature is doing it for him, sustaining his life. He is not the dreamer; he is merged with the dream of his Creator.

SONG OF THE PROPHET
TO THE SAN JUAN RIVER

That flowing water! That flowing water!
My mind wanders across it.
That broad water! That flowing water!
My mind wanders across it.
That ancient water! That flowing water!
My mind wanders across it.

Anonymous translation

Notes

The repetition of the phrase *"My mind wanders across it"* gives a sense of the relaxed state of mind of the prophet who is the singer of this traditional song. In the prophet's broad and relaxed gaze, there is a feeling similar to the gazing and gazing of the Tibetan Buddhist in Dzogchen meditation, the open-eyed gaze "like the ocean"[15]. As the prophet gazes, there is an unspoken understanding that his mind takes on the qualities of the water. In being *"flowing"*, it surrenders to the flow and journeys to levels of increasing depth. In being *"broad"*, it borders on unboundedness. In being *"ancient"*, it extends towards eternity. This is what makes the gazing a prophet's gaze.

Have you ever taken the time to gaze quietly at a brook or a river, at a lake or an ocean? The refreshing air refines the mood of the mind, and the play of sunlight on the water captures the attention and evokes associations of an eternal sparkle. In this dreamy, inspiring state, poetic associations come easily. One can sympathize with the prophet's appreciation of the river in his song.

---

15. Sogyal Rinpoche, *Dzogchen & Padmasambhava* (Berkeley: Rigpa Fellowship, 1989), p. 15.

GEORGE HERBERT
(England, 1593-1633)

PRAYER

Prayer the Churches banquet, Angels age,
  God breath in man returning to his birth,
  The soul in paraphrase, heart in pilgrimage,
The Christian plummet sounding heav'n and earth;
Engine against th'Almightie, sinners towre,
  Reversed thunder, Christ-side-piercing spear,
  The six-daies world transposing in an houre,
A kinde of tune, which all things heare and fear;
Softnesse, and peace, and joy, and love, and blisse,
  Exalted Manna, gladnesse of the best,
  Heaven in ordinaire, man well drest,
The milkie way, the bird of Paradise,
  Church-bels beyond the starres heard,
      the souls bloud,
  The land of spices; something understood.

Notes

In *Prayer*, Herbert uses a religious vocabulary and religious imagery to describe an inner experience. His description is brimming with the delights of meditation. Here are the parallels between Herbert's prayer and experiences that may occur in meditation:

"banquet": a feeling of sustenance and abundance.

"god breath in man": pranic energy or spirit.

"returning to his birth": original nature, pristine self.

"the soul in paraphrase": consciousness of the soul.

"heart in pilgrimage": journeying to new levels of being, with devotion.

"sounding heav'n and earth": plumbing the heights and depths as consciousness expands.

"Engine against th'Almightie, sinners towre, Reversed thunder": a way of impacting the divine level.

"The six-daies world transposing in an houre, ": an experience of timelessness and everything present at once.

"A kinde of tune, which all things heare and fear; ": the cosmic hum, which is the sound of the laws of nature in operation or the vibrations which structure creation.

"Softnesse, and peace": purity and inner peace.

"joy, and love, and blisse": the bliss of meditation.

"Exalted Manna": sustenance from on high; also, in meditation, the body produces substances conducive to a refined state of functioning.

"Heaven in ordinaire, man well drest": the integration of a higher state and ordinary functioning.

"The milkie way": a cosmic feeling.

"the bird of Paradise": a feeling of paradise.

"Church-bels beyond the starres heard": perception of celestial tones, a subtle sensation of inner sense.

"the souls bloud": living essence of the soul.

"The land of spices": perception of celestial fragrance or an exotic realm. (India and China supplied spices.)

something understood: metaphysical knowledge.

RAINER MARIA RILKE
(Europe, in German, 1875-1926)[16]

IF ONLY THERE WERE STILLNESS

If only there were stillness, full, complete.
If all the random and approximate
were muted, with neighbors' laughter, for your sake,
and if the clamor that my senses make
did not confound the vigil I would keep—

Then in a thousandfold thought I could
think you out, even to your utmost brink,
and (while a smile endures) possess you,
giving you away, as though I were
but giving thanks, to all the living.

Translated by Babette Deutsch

---

16. Rilke grew up in Prague at a time when it was part of the Austro-Hungarian Empire and had a German-speaking enclave. As an adult, Rilke preferred to live in France, Switzerland and Italy, although circumstances led him to spend some years in Germany and Austria.

Notes

If the reader substitutes the word God for the word *"you"* in this poem, the meaning of the poem will become apparent.

The poet wishes for complete *"stillness"*, a meditative quietness within himself and a quiet environment so that his *"senses"* will not be distracted by *"neighbors' laughter"* and all the other *"random"* input of the world.

In stillness, the poet is quite sure that he will be able to sense God, to *"think you out, even to your utmost brink"*. The connection between stillness and knowing God is inevitable. When the body and breath are still, correspondingly the mind becomes still. When the mind is still, awareness is nothing other than itself, pure awareness. That pure awareness is not just a specific, individualized phenomenon; it has a nonspecific aspect that transcends the individual, an aspect that is universal and that reflects the universal consciousness of the transcendent God.

The experience of God brings bliss, *"a smile"*. In that state of bliss, *"while a smile endures"*, the poet takes on a state of spirituality, which he describes as to *"possess"* God. In that state, he can radiate spirituality, *"giving"* God, as he passes on to others the spiritual favor that God has given him *"as though I were but giving thanks, to all the living"*.

This poem is from a collection that Rilke called *The Book of Hours* (in German *Das Stunden-Buch*), alluding to the medieval *Book of Hours* that was a collection of inspirational reflections and prayers for the hours of the day.

RABINDRANATH TAGORE
(India, in Bengali and English, 1861-1941)

GITANJALI (CIII)[17]

In one salutation to thee, my God, let all my senses spread out and touch this world at thy feet.

Like a rain-cloud of July hung low with its burden of unshed showers let all my mind bend down at thy door in one salutation to thee.

Let all my songs gather together their diverse strains into a single current and flow to a sea of silence in one salutation to thee.

Like a flock of homesick cranes flying day and night back to their mountain nests let all my life take its voyage to its eternal home in one salutation to thee.

Translated by Rabindranath Tagore

---

17. CIII (number 103) is the concluding poem in the *Gitanjali* collection.

Notes

Poet, playwright, novelist, master of the short story, composer, artist, educator and philosopher, Rabindranath Tagore is revered in India both for his genius and his spirituality. He wrote in his native language of Bengali, later translating some of his poetry into English. In the West, he received the Nobel Prize, for poems that deeply moved his fellow poets, among them W. B. Yeats and Ezra Pound.

His life integrated the accomplishment of a cultural leader with a personal piety. As a spiritual practice, daily from three to five o'clock in the morning, he sat motionless in contemplation of the divine.[18] His poems reveal his familiarity with his own soul and the spirit of God. In Nature he saw a sublime radiance. In the world he found joy and tender concern.

In the selection presented here from *Gitanjali (Song Offerings)*, Tagore pours out his desire to bow down to God, not merely physically in the Indian manner of devotion but with all his being. First he offers his physical *"senses"*; let them abandon their limited focus and spread out into the unboundedness of the divine and find their goal at the feet of God. Then he offers all his *"mind"*; let it bend down at the door of God. Next he offers all the output of his creativity, his *"songs"*, to merge into the transcendent silence of God. Finally he offers all his *"life"* and the destiny of his soul, to take its eternal rest in God.

---

18. Many religions hold the quiet hours before dawn to be conducive to contemplation.

KAROL WOJTYLA, POPE JOHN PAUL II
(Poland, 1920-)

SHORES OF SILENCE

1

The distant shores of silence begin
at the door. You cannot fly there
like a bird. You must stop, look deeper,
still deeper, until nothing deflects the soul
from the deepmost deep.

No greenery can now satisfy your sight:
the captive eyes will not come home.
And you thought life would hide you from
the other Life that overhangs the depths.

You must know – there is no return
from this flow, this embrace within the mysterious
beauty of Eternity.
Only endure, endure, do not interrupt
the flight of shadows – only endure
clear and simple – more and more.

Meanwhile you always step aside for Someone
from beyond,
who closes the door of your small room.
His coming softens with each step
and with this silence strikes
the target of the depths.

Translated by Jerzy Peterkiewicz

Notes

In 1978, Karol Wojtyla became Pope John Paul II. Almost thirty years earlier, he began his work as a poet, publishing poems anonymously in Communist Poland under the pen name of Andrzej Jawien, while his public career continued to be that of a priest.

The journey to *"the shores of silence"* begins with a paradox; it is a journey to a *"distant"* realm, and yet that realm begins at *"the door of your small room"*. It is distant because it is other-worldly; it is near because it is within your room, within you. It is not found by journeying outward but by stopping, turning inward and looking deep.

We chose this poem for its candid description of the less glamorous side of meditation, the journey of enduring. *"Only endure, endure, do not interrupt/ the flight of shadows——"*. Often the meditative state is not sensational or even blissful. It is a state of purification in which the *"shadows"* of the stress of past impressions are released from the mind and body. This purification is brought about by the orderliness of the state of *"silence"*. If one endures this boring phase, a time of clarity and delight will come. As the shadows are cleared away, one's awareness extends to new depths.

The last stanza changes the direction of the journey by stepping aside for *"Someone."* The introduction of a separate, divine Person distinguishes this poem as a religious experience.

List of Poems in Chapter Four

Dover Beach
by Matthew Arnold

Below Freezing
by Tomas Tranströmer

How Sweet the Moonlight
by William Shakespeare

The World Is Too Much with Us
by William Wordsworth

Alto Song
by Hilary Huttner

Untitled
by Juan Ramón Jiménez

Excerpt from Milarepa Tells His Story
by Milarepa

Untitled
by Han-shan

4

THE DANGER OF IGNORANCE

Ignorance is the opposite of enlightenment. To understand enlightenment, it is helpful to understand the state of ignorance that precedes it. Spiritual ignorance does not come from a lack of information but from a lack of mature consciousness. Ignorance is a developmental state of mind that is out-grown through personal spiritual experience.

Our assessment of reality depends upon our state of mind. The raw input of our senses is focused through the lens of consciousness. If the band of our awareness is narrow, if our attention is captivated by the boundaries of finite things, then the mind will miss the larger, subtler picture of the unifying wholeness of life and the spirit that animates it. The mind will miss the infinite value underlying the finite, and as a result the finite will never seem totally satisfying.

In ignorance, people know that they are conscious, but they do not perceive the nature of their own consciousness. Unfamiliar with the spiritual dimension of their personality, they do not sense their own soul nor the universal soul of God. They have no personal experience of a spiritual wholeness, of a universal essence, of something constant beyond the changes, of some intelligent, organizing power. Ignorant of how to draw on that power, even ignorant that they are spiritually malnourished, they are overwhelmed by stress and succumb to disease and other problems. Unaware of their unity with other people and with all of creation, they do not love their neighbor nor their environment as themselves, and so they are tempted to exploit them. Misguided behavior and suffering have their root in spiritual ignorance.

The symptoms of the state of ignorance are well known; they are the symptoms of the malaise of modern life. Western poets bemoan the pain of ignorance in their poems. In America, Allen Ginsberg cried out in his poem *Howl*, *"Solitude! Filth! Ugliness! Ashcans and unobtainable dollars! . . . Old men weeping in the parks!"* In England, Matthew Arnold wrote of the human plight in *Dover Beach*:

And we are here as on a darkling plain,
Swept with confused alarms of struggle and flight,
Where ignorant armies clash by night.

The *"confused alarms of struggle and flight"* are the 'fight or flight' symptoms of stress. The vicious cycle of stress keeps a person in the grip of ignorance. When accumulated stress overwhelms a person, the less-than-full functioning of the physiology results in less-than-full consciousness. That constricted consciousness produces narrow-minded behavior, which runs aground and creates more stress. Ironically, the more stressed a person is, the more difficulty he has in tearing his attention away from whatever distresses him. Thus ignorance finds a home in some of the most intelligent people.

The modern Swedish poet Tomas Tranströmer saw that not only individuals but also whole societies suffer from stress and ignorance. Just as a forest turns green or bare with the cycle of the individual trees in the forest, so human society and human history reflect the collective consciousness of their individual members. *"The unaware forest of flickering faces"* is how Tranströmer, in his poem *Below Freezing*, described his spiritually depressed society in Sweden. He also had an insightful term for stress and the *"confused alarms of struggle and flight"* that go along with it. He called it *"repressed violence"*.

Worse, in the state of ignorance, a human being is out of touch with the divine order. *"For this, for every thing, we are out of tune;"* lamented Wordsworth in his poem *The World Is Too Much with Us*. There is a lack of harmony with humankind and with Nature. Uncoordinated with the Way of life, an individual's life and the collective life of his whole society flounder in mistakes, suffering and negativity.

How did life become mired in ignorance? Here are the poets' answers:

Matthew Arnold's answer is a loss of faith, depicted in the *"long, withdrawing roar"* of the *"sea of faith"*. This seems likely, but what caused the loss of faith?

Tomas Tranströmer does not give a direct answer in his poem *Below Freezing*, but he does point out the repressed violence, the lack of love, the unaware faces, and the lack of prayer for the children in his society. He paints a picture of life choked by stress, yet he will not give up hope for a spot of illumination.

In his play *The Merchant of Venice*, Shakespeare attributes ignorance to an inadequacy in human make-up, particularly the limited senses and the crude, mortal physiology which clothes the immortal soul:

> *Such harmony is in immortal souls;*
> *But whilst this muddy vesture of decay*
> *Doth grossly close it in, we cannot hear it.*

A different answer by Wordsworth strikes at the heart of industrialized society. Wordsworth blames spiritual ignorance on a separation from nature and an over-fascination with material life. Wordsworth warned us a hundred and eighty years ago, in *The World Is Too Much with Us*, that our worship of material life would be our undoing:

> *Getting and spending, we lay waste our powers.*

Little we see in Nature that is ours.

Wordsworth saw society becoming pre-occupied with the materialism brought on by industrialization, which was allowed to ride rough-shod over the needs of spiritual life. The results of laying waste our powers are depicted with pain-filled detail in *Howl*, Allen Ginsberg's landmark poem of twentieth century angst.

Howl captures the horror of the Age of Ignorance. It is the horror of matter triumphing over spirit, the *"sphinx of cement and aluminum"* that crushed the sensitive minds of Ginsberg's generation. It is the horror of machines, buildings, governments, commerce, industrialization and social order gone wrong, so that they grind down the human spirit instead of serving it. It is a nightmarish environment, an *"incomprehensible prison"*, which *"frightened me out of my natural ecstasy"*. It drove some *"angelheaded hipsters"* to drugs, some to psychiatric hospitals, some to suicide and some to the living death of conformity with the *"robot-consciousness"* of Moloch, the personification of the loveless, ignorant group-consciousness from which Ginsberg sought liberation.

In *Alto Song* by Hilary Huttner, the necessity for participation in the daily grind drags the mind into the common denominator of ignorant life. Yet in solitude the soul may emerge to know its true nature.

Then the soul breathes silence,
And the body falls away,
And the greatness of the silence
Shames the cares of the day.

The Spanish poet Juan Ramón Jiménez, a keen observer of his own inner life, saw the dilemma most clearly as an inner mental state. He believed that ignorance would in time pass as ephemerally as a passing mood.

The black day was close to ending,
muddled in dank misery . . .
—But, inside, reality
smiling, awaited us—

The tantric poet Milarepa taught that the results of past actions and *"preconceived obsessive emotions"* clouded the mind, obscured the true nature of the self and reality, and led human beings to entangle themselves in a web of misguided action and reaction.

The poet who denounces the ignorance of his age may be considered a crackpot by the folks caught up in it. Each side has the craziness of its own perspective, as the Chinese poet Han-shan notes with a sense of humor:

The things we say he doesn't understand;
The things he says we wouldn't utter!

But Han-shan offers a way out. It is to experience what he has experienced, to visit the realm of his spiritual mountain, to observe nature and sit in meditation, to transcend the life of the village below, and thus to share the elevated perspective from his mountain vista. *"Try coming to Cold Mountain sometime!"* he calls out to people who want to wake up.

To come out of ignorance, you have to come to Cold Mountain yourself. Reading about it is not enough, just as reading about sleep will not give you rest. For personal knowledge, you must take a vacation from the stressful distractions of your everyday life and journey beyond the boundaries of ignorance. Given the freedom to seek its highest, deepest nature, the mind will expand to the infinite and return to discriminate the finite, again and again, until the mind is flexible enough to comprehend both at once, and, remembering its pure nature, is enlightened.

MATTHEW ARNOLD
(England, 1822-1888)

DOVER BEACH

The sea is calm tonight,
The tide is full, the moon lies fair
Upon the straits;— on the French coast the light
Gleams and is gone; the cliffs of England stand,
Glimmering and vast, out in the tranquil bay.
Come to the window, sweet is the night-air!
Only, from the long line of spray
Where the sea meets the moon-blanched land,
Listen! You hear the grating roar
Of pebbles which the waves draw back, and fling,
At their return, up the high strand,
Begin, and cease, and then again begin,
With tremulous cadence slow, and bring
The eternal note of sadness in.

Sophocles long ago
Heard it on the Aegean, and it brought
Into his mind the turbid ebb and flow
Of human misery; we
Find also in the sound a thought,
Hearing it by this distant northern sea.

The sea of faith
Was once, too, at the full, and round earth's shore
Lay like the folds of a bright girdle furled.
But now I only hear
Its melancholy, long, withdrawing roar,

Retreating, to the breath
Of the night-wind, down the vast edges drear
And naked shingles of the world.

Ah, love, let us be true
To one another! for the world, which seems
To lie before us like a land of dreams,
So various, so beautiful, so new,
Hath really neither joy, nor love nor light,
Nor certitude, nor peace, nor help for pain;
And we are here as on a darkling plain,
Swept with confused alarms of struggle and flight,
Where ignorant armies clash by night.

Notes

Dover Beach opens with a scene of peace and beauty but ends on a note of despair. On this night when *"the moon lies fair"*, what is there to cause *"the eternal note of sadness"*? It is the *"ebb and flow of human misery"* and the *"confused alarms of struggle and flight"*.

Arnold describes a world out of touch with divine benevolence. It is tempted by *"a land of dreams, so beautiful"* but ignorant of how to establish itself in that beauty. It is life in ignorance. Arnold associates this misery with the retreat of *"the sea of faith"*, which he believes once girded life on Earth but now is *"retreating...down the... naked shingles of the world"*.

TOMAS TRANSTRÖMER
(Sweden, 1931-)

BELOW FREEZING

We are at a party that doesn't love us. Finally the party lets the mask fall and shows what it is: a shunting station for freight cars. In the fog, cold giants stand on their tracks. A scribble of chalk on cardoors.

One can't say it aloud, but there is a lot of repressed violence here. That is why the furnishings seem so heavy. And why it is so difficult to see the other thing present: a spot of sun that moves over the house walls and slips over the unaware forest of flickering faces, a biblical saying never set down: "Come unto me, for I am as full of contradictions as you."

I work the next morning somewhere else. I drive there in a hum through the dawning hour which resembles a dark blue cylinder. Orion hangs over the frost. Children stand in a silent clump, waiting for the schoolbus, the children no one prays for. The light grows as gradually as our hair.

Translated by Robert Bly

Notes

How well Tranströmer describes the daily dreariness of urban life. His poem is appropriate for many towns beyond his native Sweden.

Tranströmer begins by pointing out a lack of love. Although the *"party that doesn't love us"* is only a foggy image of a party of trains, it makes a statement about the society to whom the trains belong. In modern societies, the members do not love one another unconditionally, and the technological inventions they depend on do not love them in return.

In lieu of love there is its opposite, *"a lot of repressed violence"*. The repressed violence clouds consciousness. Tranströmer notes two effects of this repressed violence: It makes it difficult to see the spot of sun (a symbol of spiritual illumination), and it is *"why the furnishings seem so heavy"*.

Do you believe Tranströmer about the furnishings? This is a key detail because it illustrates that the repressed violence is not just a psychological experience; it affects the physical world, too. Tranströmer points out a causal connection between the stressful atmosphere of human consciousness and the manifestation of physical reality. He does not explain it, but there is an esoteric explanation. If you believe that everything, the atoms in the furniture and even the atoms in you at their most fundamental level are constituted of a universal field of consciousness, and if you believe that everything is connected through that field, then you would conclude that the same stress which causes a gross human consciousness could also cause a grossness in the material environment. Tranströmer calls this grossness *"heavy"*, which aptly describes the impression it makes on an observer.

WILLIAM SHAKESPEARE
(England, 1564-1616)

HOW SWEET THE MOONLIGHT

How sweet the moonlight sleeps upon this bank!
Here we will sit and let the sounds of music
Creep in our ears: soft stillness and the night
Become the touches of sweet harmony.
Sit, Jessica. Look how the floor of heaven
Is thick inlaid with patines of bright gold:
There's not the smallest orb which thou behold'st
But in his motion like an angel sings,
Still quiring to the young-eyed cherubins.
Such harmony is in immortal souls;
But whilst this muddy vesture of decay
Doth grossly close it in, we cannot hear it.

From The Merchant of Venice

Notes

This famous excerpt is from Shakespeare's play *The Merchant of Venice,* Act V, scene 1, lines 54-65.

The *"muddy vesture of decay"* is the mortal body. Could this vesture be cleaned during our lifetime, so that we could appreciate the cosmic harmony? There are practices, such as meditation, yoga and other methods of purification, which hold out hope that the windows of perception can be cleaned and that the human being can find full maturity in the perception of the sublime. Shakespeare, however, implies that one must wait until the soul is free of the vesture of the body. Then the *"harmony"* in the immortal soul will be revealed. Shakespeare imagines it akin to the harmony of the heavens.

The *"orb"* which *"like an angel sings"* refers to the planetary 'music of the spheres', also known as the harmony of the spheres. This concept would have come down to Shakespeare from the ancient Greeks. In the sixth century B. C., the Ionian philosopher and mathematician Pythagorus may have referred to hearing 'the music of the heavens'. His disciples assumed that planetary ratios gave rise to a harmony analogous to the intervals on a musical instrument. Plato in his Republic described sirens on concentric rings of the cosmos singing in harmony. Add to this the Biblical vision of angelic hosts singing hymns of praise to God, and Shakespeare's picture of heavenly orbs quiring (choiring) to angelic cherubins is complete.

WILLIAM WORDSWORTH
(England, 1770-1850)

THE WORLD IS TOO MUCH WITH US

The world is too much with us; late and soon,
Getting and spending, we lay waste our powers.
Little we see in nature that is ours;
We have given our hearts away, a sordid boon!
This Sea that bares her bosom to the moon;
The winds that will be howling at all hours,
And are up-gathered now like sleeping flowers;
For this, for every thing, we are out of tune;
It moves us not.——Great God! I'd rather be
A pagan suckled in a creed outworn;
So might I, standing on this pleasant lea,
Have glimpses that would make me less forlorn;
Have sight of Proteus rising from the sea;
Or hear old Triton blow his wreathèd horn.

Notes

The Industrial Revolution struck England in the late eighteenth century. Wordsworth experienced firsthand the shift from an agrarian to an industrial civilization. His words of warning are as apt for our mature industrialized society as they were for his toddling one. Mass production requires mass consumption, which leads to a life of getting and spending rather than a life focused on the natural world and the spirit that animates it.

What would happen if the first four lines of Wordsworth's poem were posted on the entrance of a modern shopping center? Why, it would be blasphemous! But if it is blasphemous in our society to say that *"getting and spending we lay waste our powers"*, then what does that say about the values of our society? Isn't it odd that our society celebrates its holidays by having sales? Is this the cherished value for which the patriots of the American Revolution pledged "our lives, our fortunes, and our sacred honor?"

Surrounded by spiritual bankruptcy, Wordsworth concludes, *"I'd rather be/ A pagan . . ."* Similarly, people today look for spiritual alternatives in the New Age to revive their connection with Nature.

HILARY HUTTNER
(United States, 1951-)

ALTO SONG

Did you brush your teeth with brighteners?
Did you buy the morning paper?
Did you smile when your big boss
Said you'd better see him later?

Take the right-hand hallway.
Take the second desk from the left.
Take the next page on your calendar
And flip it like all the rest.

Buy the hot dogs on your way home.
Buy the instant banana surprise.
Buy the soda with only one calorie
That tastes like it has ninety-five.

But when the day is over,
When it's time to sleep,
When you lie in bed and all's been said,
When you breathe slow and deep,

Then the soul breathes silence,
And the body falls away,
And the greatness of the silence
Shames the cares of the day.

I am the deep breath of your life.
This is my alto song:
I fill the Earth, I fill the stars,
And I go on and on.

I never was a woman,
I never was a man,
I never was young or old,
I am that I am.

"Alto" in Spanish means both deep and high. When the mind picks up the characteristic sensation of sensing its own transcendent nature, its own soul, there is a feeling of going deep, almost like diving underwater and at the same time there is a feeling of exaltation, as though one were thinking on a higher plane.

Alto Song begins with the captivity of material life. The daily grind captures the attention of the mind so that it forgets its own nature. The hapless individual succumbs to social pressure to conform to the falsity and pettiness of modern life.

Yet, when the pressure and distraction are ameliorated in the quiet of the night, the person's inner nature, the soul, is revealed. The unadvertised soul makes its claim to be more important than any aspect of material life; it claims, *"I am the deep breath of your life"*. The word *"breath"* is used in two ways. First, it is used as an animating principle, as is the biblical breath by which God breathed life into Adam and the pranic energy which is the Yogic breath of life. Second, the breath is used to indicate the physiological state of the slow, deep breathing that leads to *"silence"*, when *"the body falls away"*.

The soul describes itself as unbounded and cosmic. This is in direct contrast to the limitations of daily life. It is beyond the basic distinctions of the individual's present life, beyond gender and age. It is amness.

The description of the soul resembles qualities usually associated with the divine, a likely resemblance if one agrees with the biblical adage that the soul is made in the image of God. The soul's conclusion, *"I am that I am"*, is the identity which God gave Moses, when He revealed that His name was a unique form of the verb 'to be', a first-person beingness, loosely rendered in an English translation by the phrase *"I am that I am"*.

JUAN RAMON JIMENEZ
(Spain, 1881-1958)

UNTITLED

We thought that everything was
broken, ruined, and stained . . .
—But, within, reality
smiled, and waited for us.

Tears, blood-stained and warm
against the frost-covered panes . . .
—But, inside, reality
smiled, and waited for us.

The black day was close to ending,
muddled in dank misery . . .
—But, inside, reality
smiling, awaited us—

Translated by Eloise Roach

Notes

Jiménez wrote many poems about the inner life of consciousness. Here he offers the perspective that the imperfection and misery of the world is not the ultimate reality and that there is another, better reality waiting to be found within us.

The *"tears"*, the *"black day"*, the *"dank misery"* are all too familiar to a life lived in ignorance. So vivid, they seem to be the real, biting reality. But are we right when *"We thought that everything was broken, ruined, and stained . . ."*? Or was that an ignorant notion?

Jiménez says there is something more, something beyond the painful imperfection of life, and that something can be found within. He says it is so real, it is reality itself. In its smiling nature, it makes light of the black day.

Thus, even while this ignorant life continues, a perspective of wisdom can develop along with it. That wisdom provides another slant on the *"muddled"* life. It is the perspective of the reality of an inner life that is immutably good, a level of existence that cannot be broken or stained, an immutable bliss, *"reality smiling"*.

The unhappy reality and the *"smiling"* reality, which we have understood as forms of ignorance and wisdom, can also be understood as forms of depression and elation. Jiménez suffered from bouts of depression as well as bouts of sublime feelings of the beauty and divineness of life. He expressed his sublime feelings in many poems of joy and an appreciation of nature that inspired him to thoughts of heightened consciousness.

MILAREPA
(Tibet, 1040 or 1052 - 1123 A.D.)

EXCERPT FROM MILAREPA TELLS HIS STORY

[Once when people asked Milarepa for instruction, he
sang a song which included this advice:]

These preconceived obsessive emotions
Are a curtain which hides high birth and freedom. . .
A massive cloud raining down mystery,
A thief who robs our virtue and assets,
The root which produces all of our faults.

To probe deep into your roots:
The ignorance and confusion are *you yourself.*
The preconceptions which are yourself
Are envoys and agents *sent by yourself. . .*

Now examine yourself closely:
You yourself have no color or form.
If sent *you* won't go. If restrained *you* don't stay.
If looked for *you* can't be seen.
If grasped for *you* can't be caught. . .

Return to your natural state without effort or distraction.
Know the way of such relaxation, fortunate ones.

Translated by Lama Kunga Rimpoche and Brian Cutillo
From Stories and Songs from the Oral Tradition
of Jetsun Milarepa

Notes

Milarepa is often called Tibet's greatest yogi or siddha. His cornucopia of verses are interspersed with prose to describe his adventurous life, his austere spiritual practices, his Tibetan Buddhist philosophy and his hard-won, secret wisdom. His songs of experience, which he is said to have composed and sung spontaneously in a beautiful voice, are a testimony to the higher states of consciousness which evolved from his Tibetan yoga and tantric practices. He roamed the countryside of Tibet, meditating in mountain caves.

The verses presented here reflect a psychological knowledge of who we think we are, who we really are, and why we find ourselves in such a fix. Like the yoga of neighboring India, Tibetan Buddhism includes a knowledge of the psychological development that practitioners encounter in their pursuit of an enlightened comprehension of the mind, the true self, and their relationship to reality.

In the mid-twentieth century, the country of Tibet was invaded and annexed by Communist China. Over a million Tibetans were killed and the remainder subjugated. The religious institutions, the backbone of Tibetan culture, were stripped of their art treasures and systematically destroyed. The rest of the world has now realized that it was a tragic mistake for China to take over Tibet. A future generation of Chinese leaders may come to agree with the rest of the world. For the time being, the Tibetan people, their culture and unique heritage of spiritual knowledge survive in refugee communities committed to education and a peaceful, decent way of life, preserving their culture and the Buddhist attitude of kindness and compassion. If you would like to provide humanitarian aid to Tibetan refugees, you may contact a charity established by the Dalai Lama: The Tibet Fund, 241 E. 32nd St., New York, NY 10016.

HAN-SHAN
(China, 8th Century)

UNTITLED

When people see the man of Cold Mountain
They all say, "There's a crackpot!"
Hardly a face to make one look twice,
His body wrapped in nothing but rags.
The things we say he doesn't understand;
The things he says we wouldn't utter!"
A word to those of you passing by—
Try coming to Cold Mountain sometime!

Translated by Burton Watson

Notes

The history of Han-shan is hazy, but a fair rendition is this: Han-shan was a Chinese Zen Buddhist, perhaps a retired scholar or minor official, who lived in a mountainous locale known as Cold Cliff. There he practiced a form of sitting meditation and wrote his poems. His first editor describes him as a legendary hermit whose poems were found written on large rocks and on the walls of buildings in the nearby village.

In Han-shan's poetry, the cold mountain is both his physical and his spiritual abode. He suggests that it is by rising to his state of mind and by experiencing what he has experienced that one can appreciate his mountaintop perspective. One has to participate in the mental experience of the cold mountain, his place of meditation. Without that perspective, he laments that what he says will seem meaningless.

His poems have a tinge of loneliness, at times despair, the joy of spiritual insight, and sometimes the crackling humor displayed in this poem.

List of Poems in Chapter Five

Untitled
by John Henry Newman

When I Am Not Dead
by John Ciardi

Shadows
by D. H. Lawrence

The Latest Freed Man
by Wallace Stevens

Full Moon
by Tu Fu

i thank You God for most this amazing
by e. e. cummings

The List
by Michael McClure

Untitled
by Joho

Untitled
by Dogen

5

AWAKENING

This chapter is about the exciting transition from old consciousness to new—the opening of the eye of consciousness—a new way of perceiving, a new world-view, a new harmony, a new self. When consciousness awakens, a constellation of changes occurs. The mind awakens, the senses awaken, the body awakens, the heart awakens, the soul awakens!

Dogen, an awakened Zen master and poet, called us ordinary folk *"dream-walkers"*. Just as we may be totally taken in by a dream, we are so totally taken in by our ordinary waking state that it is hard to imagine that we could wake up from it into some greater reality. Yet people do wake up from it. The poets and sages have reported it in their writings. And in their enlightened awakening, there is the same sense of relief, freedom and understanding that we experience when we wake up from a bad dream.

The poems in this chapter are about what it feels like to awaken—the freedom, the aliveness, the refreshment, the bliss, the new appreciation of the world. The chapter begins with the mystifying little awakenings that are signs of the development of consciousness and progresses to the emphatic declarations of the fully awakened Zen masters. Later chapters explore the wisdom that comes with awakening — an awareness of one's Self, of the essence of things, of God, and of the unity which unifies Self, world and God.

There are at least eight common metaphors for awakening: 1) to open your eyes or the eye of knowledge; 2) to wake up from a sleep or dream; 3) to blossom or grow like a flower or plant; 4) to be born, reborn or to come alive from being dull or dead; 5) to come into the light; 6) to start a new day or a new season; 7) to become clear of obstacles or impurities; and 8) to be freed or liberated from an old condition. Using these metaphors, Newman wakes up with *"a strange refreshment"* and *"a sense of freedom"*. Ciardi writes about *"when I am not dead"*, and Lawrence finds *"new blossoms of me"*. Steven's man is *"freed"* at dawn. McClure *"relaxes into new birth"*. Joho sees *"without an obstacle in sight"*. Dogen is *"awakened"* to hear *"the one true thing"*.

To awaken is to become more aware, more aware of one's self and more aware of the spiritual basis of reality. For some people, adult awareness matures into a subtle sense of an absolute, witnessing self and a subtle appreciation of the intelligence which governs life. This subtle awareness is the beginning of enlightenment, which is consciousness awakening to itself. Enlightenment is individual consciousness awakening to its own soul and to the soul of existence, which are both the same creative intelligence, the essence which is at the basis of everything. The subtle awareness of this spiritual omnipresence, within and without, is the vision that Joho wanted to communicate in his poem when he declared, *"It's everywhere!"*

The development of enlightenment has been mapped in detail in the traditions of India, Tibet and Asia. For example, in the Vedic science expounded by Maharishi Mahesh Yogi, enlightenment is understood to progress through three stages: 1) a liberating awareness of the absolute nature of the inner Self, 2) an awareness of the absolute omnipresence which gives a glorious value to the manifested world and which inspires the heart with devotion, and 3) a unifying awareness which recognizes that the absolute nature of the inner self and the absolute nature of the outer world are expressions of one unified field of pure consciousness. The philosophies of the East have practices to foster enlightenment which are intended to develop the individual more systematically and more quickly than haphazard maturation.

Rare is awakening into full enlightenment. Yet a knowledge of this potential enables a person to understand the little awakenings that are its harbingers. As consciousness expands, new experiences become possible. These experiences may be moments of intuitive knowledge as cognition expands, feelings of happiness as the capacity for bliss expands, glorious sensory perception as the channels of the senses are cleared, good health and energy as the body functions more efficiently, freedom as a sense of the unassailable Self develops, harmony between the individual and the environment as a sense of unity emerges, or a closeness with God and divine order as spirituality deepens. Such experiences are reported in the writings of many poets; a slew of them can be found in Newman's untitled poem in this chapter.

Moments of awakening may come and go, as enlightenment develops in patches. The contrast of slipping from heightened awareness back to the ordinary waking state is a common lament. Both Ciardi and Lawrence describe the contrast in their poems. Ciardi writes: *"When I am not dead I/ see and can remember/ everything...and then I do die/ and do not know I have/ died..."* Lawrence likened the contrast to the phases of the moon and the changes of the season. He understood that the winter of the spirit was a time of preparation that would result in a new inner life blossoming in the spring.

and still, among it all, snatches of lovely oblivion,
*   and snatches of renewal*
odd, wintry flowers upon the withered stem,
*   yet new, strange flowers*
such as my life has not brought forth before. . .

As consciousness grows, one's perception of the outer world also blossoms. Reality is perceived more fully, more subtly and more gloriously from the perspective of heightened awareness. The poet looks closely at a leaf, and a deeper reality zooms into view. Wallace Stevens, whose poems show much inner development, says in *The Latest Freed Man*:

It was everything being more real, himself
At the centre of reality, seeing it.
It was everything bulging and blazing and big
       in itself . . .

This brilliant world-view dawns when the nervous system is clear and flexible enough to accommodate the glory of what it is perceiving, when it is no longer knotted by the impressions of past stresses, and when the whole continuum of mind and body is in a state of Buddha-like ease. Then the senses come alive. The ordinary looks divine because its divine value is appreciated. e. e. cummings gave thanks for it: *"i thank you God for most this amazing/ day . . . which is natural which is infinite which is yes"*.

Because the mind and body have correlated states, as the mind awakens into the state of perfection, the body also evolves towards perfect functioning. Freedom from mental burdens is accompanied by a feeling of lightness in the body. Unencumbered, the body becomes less destructible, the metabolism more efficient, the breath quieter, the nervous system calmer, the senses more sensitive. The body becomes impervious to stress, which has no more effect than the proverbial line drawn on water, and thus the body remains refreshed and the aging process is minimized. The physical sensations of awakening into an experience of higher consciousness have been described by Cardinal Newman:

I went to sleep; and now I am refreshed,
A strange refreshment: for I feel in me
An inexpressible lightness, and a sense
Of freedom, as if I were at length myself,
And ne'er had been before. How still it is!
I hear no more the busy beat of time,
No, nor my fluttering breath, nor struggling pulse;
Nor does one moment differ from the next.
                                    . . . now I am
So whole of heart, so calm, so self-possessed. . .

The change in consciousness from ordinary wakefulness (in which the mind is awake to the outer world) to a
higher state of wakefulness (in which the mind is awake
both to the outer world and to its own and universal consciousness) is as dramatic as a rebirth.   Michael McClure
gives us this view in his poem *The List*:

> *These all speak more*
> *as our stiff-*
> *ness re-*
> *laxes*
> *into new birth.*
> *The worth*
> *of things*
> *cracks open*
> *and shows*
> *the intestines.*

Awakening is a time of greater self-actualization and a
greater understanding of reality. It involves the whole person, the intellect, the emotions, the senses, the body. The
poems make it clear that awakening is an experience of
personal growth and that enlightenment is not something
that is learned.

93

As you awaken yourself, you will catch the allusions to awakening in the writings of many people. The Zen monks who preserved their mystical insights in short poems knew that only a few words were needed to signal their enlightenment to like-minded readers. Yet the same writings may appear nonsensical to readers who have not had some similar personal experience. How many generations have been pleased and puzzled by this cryptic statement by Zen master Dogen:

Awakened, I hear the one true thing—
Black rain on the roof of Fukakusa Temple.

JOHN HENRY NEWMAN
(England, 1801-1890)

UNTITLED

I went to sleep; and now I am refreshed,
A strange refreshment: for I feel in me
An inexpressible lightness, and a sense
Of freedom, as if I were at length myself,
And ne'er had been before. How still it is!
I hear no more the busy beat of time,
No, nor my fluttering breath, nor struggling pulse;
Nor does one moment differ from the next. . . .
Another marvel: some one has me fast
Within his ample palm; 'tis not a grasp
Such as they use on earth, but all around
Over the surface of my subtle being,
As though I were a sphere and capable
To be accosted thus; a uniform
And gentle pressure tells me I am not
Self-moving, but borne forward on my way.
And hark! I hear a singing; yet in sooth
I cannot of that music rightly say
Whether I hear or touch or taste the tones.
Oh, what a heart-subduing melody! . . .
Now know I surely that I am at length
Out of the body: had I part with earth,
I never could have drunk those accents in,
And not have worshipped as a God that voice
That was so musical; but now I am
So whole of heart, so calm, so self-possessed,
With such a full content, and with a sense
So apprehensive and discriminate,
As no temptation can intoxicate.
Nor have I even terror at the thought
That I am clasped by such a saintliness.

Notes

Here is an experience that is bound to please New Agers, yet it was written by a Victorian English cardinal. Every line of this poem has something interesting:

"A strange refreshment" is a common effect of a meditative state, and it persists as enlightenment grows. The refreshment is brought about partly by the deep rest that the body enjoys when the breath, pulse and other functions become still (*"how still"*), partly by the release of mental burdens and physical stress, and partly by spiritual expansion.

There is a sense of liberation and of returning to one's original nature. In *"freedom"*, one becomes one's pure, unencumbered self, *"as if I were at length myself/ And ne'er had been before"*.

Accompanying the sense of liberation is a sense of not being as weighed down as before. The feeling of *"an inexpressible lightness"* is a common spiritual experience. There is a spiritual unburdening and more energy to move the body.

"How still it is!" exclaims Newman. Yet the stillness is integrated with his active mind. Such integration is another sign of enlightenment, in which the changeless, absolute state is united with the realm of activity. The timeless Absolute causes time to lose its sting: *"I hear no more the busy beat of time. . . Nor does one moment differ from the next . . ."*

"Another marvel: some one has me fast/ Within his ample palm . . ." This is a reference to being in the hand of God, a description that has a special realism as Newman describes it *"over the surface of my subtle being,/ As though I were a sphere"*.

Next comes an experience of celestial perception in the form of heavenly music. This is enriched by synesthesia, a mixture of the senses. Newman writes:

And hark! I hear a singing; yet in sooth
I cannot of that music rightly say
Whether I hear or touch or taste the tones.

The fact that Newman could not tell *"whether I hear or touch or taste the tones"* indicates that his mind was functioning on a subtle level of inner experience, as indeed it would have to be to appreciate the subtle, divine glory. On that subtle level, at which thoughts are apprehended soon after they emerge in a compact form, the branches of the senses come together, making possible a joint contribution to the apprehension of a sound. The vocabulary of music reflects the contribution of all senses, such as when music is soaring (kinesthesia), sweet (taste), smooth (feeling), or dark (sight). So it is not surprising that Newman felt the celestial tones or tasted their sweetness as much as he heard them.[3]

Newman goes on, *"Now know I surely that I am at length/ Out of the body:"* Although it is not necessary to be out of the body to have such experiences, Newman concludes that he was. In the most dramatic form of out-of-the-body experience, the mind, enrobed in a subtle body, floats above the gross physical body and may look down upon it. Because Newman does not report seeing his body as separate from himself, it may be that Newman is referring to a less physical experience, more of a mental disengagement from the gross limitations of the body.

The effect of the whole experience is salubrious and fulfilling. Newman finds himself *"So whole of heart, so calm, so self-possessed,/ With such a full content . . ."* that he has no fear of the extraordinary awakening which has befallen him.

---

3. For more information about the celestial perception of music, see the notes to the poems *God's Harp* and *Tea at the Palaz of Hoon.*

JOHN CIARDI
(United States, 1916-1986)

WHEN I AM NOT DEAD

When I am not dead I
see and can remember
everything. I am able
and well-feasted. I
can go to anything
for it to happen, or
wait for it to come.
I know your name deep
as you wait to know
it. I am there wait-
ing and being your
name. I can say sun
and the shadow of all
names in it. I can
count fishes by rings
on a ripple. I love
and am instantly be-
lievable and can wait
for every instant I
am

and then I do die
(the telephone rings,
a car stops, a calend-
ar clicks into an air-
plane and fastens its
seat-belt, the host-
ess smiles, I talk to
salesmen and get off)
and do not know I have
died and do not know

even that I am waiting
    until instantly
sometimes I am again
not dead and I see and
can remember every-
thing I am, and your
name, and sun, and our
shadow in it and that
I was always (and did
not know it) waiting.

Notes

    "Dead" is Ciardi's word for the dull awareness of his ordinary consciousness. When he is not dead, he has a delightful higher awareness. Then he remembers who he really is. He is fulfilled, *"well-feasted"* and *"able"*. With the expansion of his heart, he can express love truly and therefore is *"instantly believable"*. He has a deeper knowledge of *"everything I am, and your name, and sun, and our shadow in it"*. The *"sun"* reminds him of a greatness that encompasses all things. Therein lies part of his own being, in a subtle way like a *"shadow"*.

    But, alas, the mundane distractions of the ordinary world pull him out of this state of fulfillment and knowledge. He finds himself winking in and out of higher consciousness. This is a common experience in the development of enlightenment. There are moments of clarity, and then some impression grips the mind or some stress overloads the physiology and obscures that clarity. Eventually, the higher awareness will become unshakable.

D. H. LAWRENCE
(England, 1885-1930)

SHADOWS

And if tonight my soul may find her peace
in sleep, and sink in good oblivion,
and in the morning wake like a new-opened flower
then I have been dipped again in God, and
        new-created.

And if, as weeks go round, in the dark of the moon
my spirit darkens and goes out, and soft strange
        gloom
pervades my movements and my thoughts and words
then I shall know that I am walking still
with God, we are close together now the moon's
        in shadow.

And if, as autumn deepens and darkens
I feel the pain of falling leaves, and stems that
        break in storms
and trouble and dissolution and distress
and then the softness of deep shadows folding,
        folding
around my soul and spirit, around my lips
so sweet, like a swoon, or more like the drowse
        of a low, sad song
singing darker than the nightingale, on, on
        to the solstice
and the silence of short days, the silence of the year,
        the shadow,

then I shall know that my life is moving still
with the dark earth, and drenched
with the deep oblivion of earth's lapse and renewal.

And if, in the changing phases of man's life
I fall in sickness and in misery,
my wrists seem broken and my heart seems dead
and strength is gone, and my life
is only the leavings of a life:

and still, among it all, snatches of lovely oblivion,
        and snatches of renewal
odd, wintry flowers upon the withered stem, yet new,
        strange flowers
such as my life has not brought forth before, new
        blossoms of me——

then I must know that still
I am in the hands of the unknown God,
he is breaking me down to his own oblivion
to send me forth on a new morning, a new man.

What a beautiful expression of faith. Like Ciardi, Lawrence describes an on-again-off-again growth of consciousness that comes in *"snatches"*. With great maturity, Lawrence understands that it is like the cycle of the full and dark moons and the passing of the seasons. At times his lot is peace, mystic oblivion and renewal; at other times gloom and distress. Yet he has the faith to see that God is with him even in the shadows and that the silence is a time of preparation in which his *"life is moving still"*. He understands the *"lovely oblivion"* to be a transcendence that is from God and from which he will waken *"on a new morning, a new man"*.

Lawrence captures the realism of spiritual growth. The moment of awakening, the *"new-opened flower"*, is the culmination of a season of preparation. That preparation is like the Winter that precedes Spring. It is a time of darkness, shadows, silence, deepness and dissolution, a time when the old life is broken down and the new life incubated in *"the deep oblivion"*. Not everyone is wise as Lawrence was to connect the winter of the spirit, the phase of purification, dissolution and waiting for maturity, with the *"new blossoms of me"* which spring up seemingly out of nowhere.

Lawrence was an esoteric thinker. He formulated his own psychological theories based on esoteric centers in the body. The biography, *D. H. Lawrence: His Life and Works,* offers some clues to his mystical background:

> *Lawrence believed that he was "only trying to stammer out the first terms of a forgotten knowledge."*
> *...Lawrence admits that he had taken suggestions from "all kinds of scholarly books, from the Yoga and Plato and St. John the Evangel and the early Greek*

philosophers like Heriakleitos down to Frazer and his Golden Bough, and even Freud and Frobenius." He says that he remembers only hints and proceeds by intuition.

Professor William York Tindall, in D. H. Lawrence and Susan His Cow, does some scholarly sleuthing to trace Lawrence's debt to the Upanishads through Mme. Blavatsky and theosophy in general...[1]

Lawrence also had friends who were interested in Eastern religion, and he stayed six weeks in Ceylon at the home of the Brewsters who were studying Buddhism.[2]

Despite these influences, the poems by Lawrence presented in this anthology do not seem to be built on borrowed ideas. They come across as original, keenly felt descriptions of a genuinely mystical life.

---

1. Harry T. Moore, *D. H. Lawrence: His Life and Works* (New York: Twayne, 1964), pp. 159-160.
2. Ibid., p. 181.

WALLACE STEVENS
(United States, 1879-1955)

THE LATEST FREED MAN

Tired of the old descriptions of the world,
The latest freed man rose at six and sat
On the edge of his bed. He said,
                              "I suppose there is
A doctrine to this landscape. Yet, having just
Escaped from the truth, the morning is color and
        mist,
Which is enough: the moment's rain and sea,
The moment's sun (the strong man vaguely seen),
Overtaking the doctrine of this landscape. Of him
And of his works, I am sure. He bathes in the mist
Like a man without a doctrine. The light he gives—
It is how he gives his light. It is how he shines,
Rising upon the doctors in their beds
And on their beds. . . ."
                              And so the freed man said.
It was how the sun came shining into his room:
To be without a description of to be,
For a moment on rising, at the edge of the bed,
        to be,
To have the ant of the self changed to an ox
With its organic boomings, to be changed
From a doctor into an ox, before standing up,
To know that the change and that the ox-like
        struggle
Come from the strength that is the strength of
        the sun,
Whether it comes directly or from the sun.
It was how he was free. It was how his freedom
        came.

It was being without description, being an ox.
It was the importance of the trees outdoors,
The freshness of the oak-leaves, not so much
That they were oak-leaves, as the way they looked.
It was everything being more real, himself
At the centre of reality, seeing it.
It was everything bulging and blazing and big
        in itself,
The blue of the rug, the portrait of Vidal,
Qui fait fi des joliesses banales, the chairs.

Notes

This poem is about the liberation of consciousness, the dawning of enlightenment. The freed man is freed from an old state of consciousness and awakens into a new, higher state.

The Latest Freed Man describes an episode of awakening with such familiarity that it must be based on some personal experience. A detail like the vitality of the oak leaves would not mean much to someone unless he had experienced the indescribable improvement that comes from looking at the world with greater consciousness.

The freshness of the oak-leaves, not so much
That they were oak-leaves, as the way they
    looked.

The poem contrasts the old with the new. It begins with a weariness of the old understanding of reality, the old *"descriptions"* of the world, the old doctrines. As in other poems by Wallace Stevens, there is a premise that reality appears differently according to the mind of the observer. When the mind is freed, reality appears more vivid and more real. Stevens' appreciative descriptions of common-place things reflect that vividness. The experience of reality becoming more real is a sign of growing enlightenment. When consciousness expands, reality is perceived more fully, more subtly and more divinely; thus reality appears more vivid, more real and more important. Watch what happens to the latest freed man:

First he awakens. There is the image of arising from bed at dawn, a literal awakening from sleep, but wait—there's more this morning. He has escaped from the old *"truth"*. Now the morning is more truly itself and is fulfilling to him; he says that it is *"enough"*. A sense of enoughness or fulfillment accompanies awakening as the mind appreciates a deeper value in existence.

The sun, a symbol of the illumination of consciousness, and the strong man, a symbol of his new self, overtake the restrictive doctrines of the old system of truth. The strong man bathes in the mist of the morning of awakening, merging with it. He is free from the old authority and the old knowledge; he is *"without a doctrine"*.

The strong, free man gives out spiritual *"light"*. It is the light of consciousness. He has risen above the *"doctors"*. (Doctors is a play on words which refers to the people caught up in doctrines.) The latest freed man can bring light to both the doctors who are still unawakened in bed and even the structure (the bed) which supports them.

The *"latest freed man"* has a new awareness of his being. It is *"To be without a description of to be"*. This is an essential, pure beingness. His small individual self (represented by *"the ant of the self"*) is transformed into a larger, stronger self, represented by an *"ox"*. He has the insight that the strength of his new self is from the strength of the *"sun"* of enlightenment.

The freed man sees the world with a new appreciation. He has a classic experience of heightened consciousness: He sees *"the importance"*. The importance is abstract to him because he is in an early stage of awakening. As consciousness grows, a person comes to understand what this metaphysical importance is. But for now, on the first morning of awakening, it is simply a new *"freshness"*.

> *It was the importance of the trees outdoors,*
> *The freshness of the oak-leaves . . .*
> *It was everything being more real . . .*

Wallace Stevens closes his poem with a bit of whimsy. In the closing scene, the portrait of Vidal seems to scorn (*"qui fait fi"*) the commonplace beauties (*"des joliesses banales"*) which have taken on a more important reality for the freed man. Such imagined scorn cannot dim the joy of the latest freed man in even the humblest objects of Reality, *"the chairs"*.

TU FU
(China, 712-770)

FULL MOON

Isolate and full, the moon
Floats over the house by the river.
Into the night the cold water rushes away below the gate.
The bright gold spilled on the river is never still.
The brilliance of my quilt is greater than precious silk.
The circle without blemish.
The empty mountains without sound.
The moon hangs in the vacant, wide constellations.
Pine cones drop in the old garden,
The senna trees bloom.
The same clear glory extends for ten thousand miles.

Translated by Kenneth Rexroth

Notes

The full moon evokes the image of a fully illumined consciousness. The clarity, brilliance and unboundedness of the moonlight convey *"the same clear glory"* of pure consciousness. As the moonlight enhances the *"quilt"*, making it more brilliant than *"precious silk"*, so a fully illumined consciousness enhances perception, making each perception more vivid, more glorious and more precious.

The completeness of the *"circle without blemish"* expresses the fullness which is at home in the quiet, expansive emptiness of the *"vacant, wide constellation"*. The number *"ten thousand"* by convention also connotes completeness, extending as far as measurable. The emptiness of the *"empty mountains"* is a form of purity.

Life is glorified: *"The brilliance of my quilt is greater than precious silk"*. Life is dynamic: *"the cold water rushes away below the gate. . . . The senna trees bloom"*. Life is unbounded and complete: *"The same clear glory extends for ten thousand miles."*

e. e. cummings
(United States, 1894-1962)

I THANK YOU GOD FOR MOST THIS AMAZING

i thank You God for most this amazing
day:for the leaping greenly spirits of trees
and a blue true dream of sky;and for everything
which is natural which is infinite which is yes

(i who have died am alive again today,
and this is the sun's birthday;this is the birth
day of life and of love and wings:and of the gay
great happening illimitably earth)

how should tasting touching hearing seeing
breathing any —lifted from the no
of all nothing —human merely being
doubt unimaginable You?

(now the ears of my ears awake and
now the eyes of my eyes are opened)

Notes

e. e. cummings did not like to use capital letters, not even for his own name, so it is quite a concession that he capitalizes the words *"You God"*. The large letters are in keeping with his great appreciation of this special day, which is so lively with infinite value that he cannot doubt God's existence.

"this amazing day" is a day of awakening, *"(now the ears of my ears awake and/ now the eyes of my eyes are opened)"*. Nothing miraculous happens outside of himself on this day; after all, the trees are green as usual, the sky is blue as usual. But inside of himself, a rebirth and expansion take place that make everything appear in a new light. The awakening of consciousness results in a greater appreciation of life because the range of appreciation is extended to the infinite value of life, *"everything/ which is natural which is infinite which is yes"*. The infinite value includes *"love"*, bliss (*"gay great happening"*), freedom from limitations (*"illimitably"*), exaltation (*"leaping"* and *"wings"*), recognition of spiritual essence (*"greenly spirits"*), a rebirth into the life most worth living (*"alive again today"*), and an appreciation of the divineness of creation which chases away any doubt about God's presence (*how should . . . human . . . doubt unimaginable You?*).

Filled with happiness and appreciation, he offers this poem in thanksgiving. It is a wonderful kind of prayer, contemporary, playful and heartfelt.

MICHAEL MCCLURE
(United States, 1932-)

THE LIST

OLD MEN SLEEPING
IN SPEEDING CARS,
a hawk on a boulder
dripping with fog,
ten deer
in an autumn meadow,
yellow
aspens,
bishop pines
by the ocean.
These all speak more
as our stiff-
ness re-
laxes
into new birth.
The worth
of things
cracks open
and shows
the intestines.

———————————

Glittering
gold
trembling
on darkness.

Notes

The *"list"* or catalog of items is a fashionable poetic form, well-suited for the realism and attention to concrete details favored by modern poets. This poem gives the list a twist by concluding with an image of the metaphysical essence of the items in the list. Above the line drawn in the poem are the tangible items; below the line is the intangible essence.

The transition from the physical to the metaphysical occurs when *"our stiffness relaxes into new birth"*. There is much wisdom about the development of consciousness in this phrase. The word *"stiffness"* characterizes a condition which is too bound up and inflexible to appreciate the sublime value of what it is exposed to. What is the cure? Relaxation with a capital R. This is not ordinary relaxation. It is letting go of the old condition. This letting go occurs spontaneously in a meditative state. Whether or not one purposefully enters such a state, some letting go, some relaxing of the old order, is essential to proceed to a new style of functioning. When one relaxes most fully, one transcends the chain of action and reaction which kept the old order going. Even relaxing a little bit softens the boundaries of awareness and makes new insights possible. The *"new birth"* that occurs when *"our stiffness relaxes"* is a new style of functioning of consciousness.

In this state of awareness, *"the worth of things"* is revealed. The *"glittering gold"* is the glory of the inner essence.

JOHO
(China, 12th Century)

UNTITLED

Fathomed at last!
Ocean's dried, Void burst.
Without an obstacle in sight,
It's everywhere!

Translated by Lucien Stryk and Takashi Ikemoto

Notes

Joho was a Zen monk. To understand his poem requires an understanding of the Ocean and the Void in the context of Zen.

In Zen writing, painting and rock gardens, the ocean may be used as a metaphor. Sometimes it is a metaphor for the human mind; sometimes it is a metaphor for the whole of reality, which is an expression of the One Mind. The ocean has levels of increasing depth: for example, the mountain peaks that jut above the surface, the active waves, the currents of the mid-depths, the silent bottom. Similarly, the human mind has levels of depth: for example, the most manifest expression of speech, the active thoughts, the less pronounced feelings, the silent transcendental consciousness. Also similar, the created world has subtler levels of manifestation: for example, the solids that we can put our hands on, the atoms which are mostly empty space, the particle-waves, the vacuum state and, the Zennists would say, the Void.

The ocean can be simultaneously silent at the deepest level and active with waves on the surface level. The waves are nothing but fluctuations of the endless ocean, and yet each wave seems to have its individuality. Similarly, all thoughts are nothing but fluctuations of consciousness, and all things, though they seem to have individual forms, are nothing but fluctuations of the endless Void of the one cosmic mind.

The Void is the transcendent source. It is also the omnipresent essence. A parallel with Western physics is helpful in picturing this. In quantum mechanics, there is an omnipresent vacuum state out of which the particle-waves manifest and into which they may disappear and be transformed. The vacuum state is empty of actual particles but filled with virtual particles. Is it correct to call it empty or full? From the viewpoint of manifest reality, it is empty. From the viewpoint of the void, it is full of the potential of all creation. Although the Void is often called Emptiness, the Buddhist *Tchag Tchen Gyi Zindi* warns, *"Do not think of the Void as being nothingness."*[4]

The Oriental concept of the Void is different from the Western concept of the vacuum state in four important respects. First, the Void is consciousness. Not *has* consciousness but *is* pure consciousness, called by Zennists the one mind, cosmic mind, original mind or Buddha-mind. Second, the Void is transcendent; therefore, it is beyond the finite theories of the vacuum state. Third, the Void underlies a continuum of mind and matter, whereas the vacuum state only underlies matter. Fourth, the Void can be experienced by the human mind. Master Hui Hai declares in *The Path to Sudden Attainment, "When the mind is detached, the Void appears."*[5]

Although unmanifest, the Void is appreciated by the enlightened seer. Because it is omnipresent, it is appreciable everywhere, in everything. This is the paradox of enlightenment: the simultaneity of the manifest and unmanifest, form and emptiness. The wave is the ocean and the ocean is the wave in one wholeness. The Buddhist *Heart Sutra* states, *"That which is form is emptiness, that which is emptiness form."*[6]

When the poet Joho says, *"Fathomed at last!/ Ocean's dried, Void burst,"* he means that his awareness has fathomed all the levels of reality (to the ocean bottom) and emptied (*"dried"*) the Ocean of the mind. Thus the ocean bottom, the silent basis of reality, is no longer hidden. He

4. Robert Linssen, *Zen: The Art of Life* (New York: Pyramid, 1972), p. 142.
5. Ibid., p. 142.
6. Anonymous translation, *The Heart Sutra* (Cambridge, Mass.: Cambridge Zen Center, 1989), p. 4.

has penetrated (*"burst"*) the Void. He has burst the illusory veil between the unmanifest and the manifest, between emptiness and form.

Now there are *"no obstacles in sight"*. The *"obstacles"* were impurities in his mind and body that impeded the clear functioning of his consciousness. Although Joho does not say explicitly how the obstacles were removed, it is assumed through his Zen meditation.

Having overcome all obstacles, the awakened Joho sees the One Mind *"everywhere"*. He sees the omnipresence of pure consciousness which, being omnipresent, is simultaneously his own consciousness and the Buddha-mind and the essence of all things. It is the same consciousness he came to know in meditation, and now he recognizes it everywhere.

What does it look like? It looks familiar, like something that was seen before many times, yet was too faintly seen to be appreciated. Everything is the same, and yet the way of apprehending is different, so that a commonality is recognized which was not recognized before. It lends to everything in which *"it"* appears a look of intelligence and a look of self-same beingness, a universal soulness, inspiring and dear.

DOGEN
(Japan, 13th Century)

UNTITLED

That slowly drifting cloud is pitiful;
What dreamwalkers men become.
Awakened, I hear the one true thing—
Black rain on the roof of Fukakusa Temple.

Translated by Lucien Stryk and Takashi Ikemoto

Notes

Dogen was a Zen master as well as a talented poet. His awakening is *satori*, the Zen enlightenment.

The translator Lucien Stryk notes that this is one of the most famous poems by Dogen. The poem presents a terse contrast between ignorance and enlightenment. Its fame, though, is probably due to the tantalizing prize it dangles—knowledge of *"the one true thing"*. As with the Zen koans, the one true thing cannot be understood from this poem if the reader is in a state of ignorance. Rather, once one understands the one true thing, then one can appreciate Dogen's poem.

The poem opens with images of life in ignorance. The cloud is a common symbol of ignorance: something of little substance and yet enough to obscure illumination. Sleeping, dreaming and *"dreamwalking"* are also metaphors of ignorance as a state of less-than-full consciousness, a state from which one is *"awakened"* in enlightenment.

In the awakened state, the poet hears what is *"true"*, in contrast to the illusory dreamwalking of other men. What is this great truth? Dogen does not give us a statement about God or a moral principle. In Zen style, he selects a commonplace slice of reality, the rain, which, being reality, can be nothing other than the omnipresent *"one true thing"*. Dogen speaks from the perspective of enlightenment, perceiving the universal in the particular.

Dogen's description of the rain is crisp; the very name of the temple, Fukakusa, sounds like the ping of rain on the roof. But beyond what Dogen reveals about his experience in this poem, there may be much more left unsaid. What does the rain sound like to an awakened mind?

We were lucky enough to have a temporary experience of hearing the one true thing in the rain, which is the consciousness in the rain. It is hearing the rain doing exactly what it is supposed to do, at exactly the right time—an expression of cosmic intelligence and yet (the strangest part) simultaneously an expression of your own intelligence. This is a wonderfully fulfilling experience, hearing every raindrop come down in the right place! That is hearing the sound of the rain! To hear the rain as a symphony being played according to plan, as though the drops were notes in a composition—your composition, your choreography, and, on a deeper level, your Self—can only be heard when the individual mind expands to the perspective of the cosmic mind. As a master teacher of Zen meditation, Dogen was in a good position to hear this delight.

List of Poems in Chapter Six

I Built My Hut
by T'ao Ch'ien

In
by Vicente Huidobro

The Heart of Secrets
by Hilary Huttner

The Breathing
by Denise Levertov

Song of Myself, 50
by Walt Whitman

City Psalm
by Denise Levertov

When you open your eyes deep in a wave
by Karol Wojtyla, Pope John Paul II

God's Grandeur
by Gerard Manley Hopkins

Untitled
by Bunan

The Word
by Richard Realf

6

ESSENCE

The idea that the essence of life can be found in both animate and inanimate existence, in all things from the minute to the grand, is an age-old proposition that seems radical each time it is rediscovered.

This chapter brings together poems that touch on the essence of life and the essential self of the human individual. The magic of the poems is that they describe this fundamental, universal essence in such a concrete way with such a common sense view that the reader is left with the feeling "Yes, I've seen that too, only I didn't know it!"

The essence of life is all around us, and it is inseparable from our existence, but what is it and what does it say about who I am? The answer that emerges from the poetic verses echoes the mystic answer of the perennial philosophy: I am That. Thou art That. All this is That. That is all there is.[1] Realize what That is, and you have the key to your deepest nature and the nature of reality.

What is That? It is *"Everlasting Thought"* declared the poet Richard Realf. In the expanded state of awareness in which human consciousness appreciates universal consciousness, the essence of existence is found to be nonmaterial, spiritual consciousness. In moments of rapture, Wordsworth knew it. In his poem *Tintern Abbey*, Wordsworth found the essence of life to be this:

A motion and a spirit, that impels
All thinking things, all objects of thought,
And rolls through all things

---

1. These are the Mahavakya, the Four Great Sentences from the Upanishads.

Through the experience of the poems, we can get a sense of the universal essence that goes deeper than definitions. It is the hidden way of things, the heart of all mystical secrets. It is as the Chilean poet Huidobro says, *"the heart that shines"*, which is *"the heart of the heart"*, which is *"in"* everything, the birds, the night, the sky.

When the mysterious heart of life, *"the heart that shines"*, is glimpsed by a poet, it inspires poetic descriptions of the most ordinary things. *The Heart of Secrets* strings together a series of experiences of the sublime nature of ordinary things. In those simple things is revealed an essence with the qualities of peace, life, infinity, glory, bliss and timelessness.

Those simple things, from the stones underfoot to the the clouds above, take on a new importance because their fundamental being is so keenly felt. It is keenly felt because it is the intimate perception of the essence that the poet has in common with everything that he or she sees. That essence is a form of consciousness or intelligence of the most general sort.

The nature of the essence comes through with a strong sense of reality in the poems of Denise Levertov, who is the grande dame of contemporary poetry. In her poem *The Breathing*, she describes the essence as:

> *So absolute, it is*
> *no other than*
> *happiness itself, a breathing*
> *too quiet to hear.*

The solitude of nature is conducive to the quiet state of mind that can reach the silent level of existence, *"the breathing too quiet to hear"*. More challenging is Ms. Levertov's poem of an urban experience, *City Psalm*, which, despite the grief of city life, attests to *"an otherness that was blesséd, that was bliss"*. That *"otherness"* is the unchanging reality persevering beneath the surface chaos of the city. It is independent of time and place.

With similar insight, in the midst of the difficulties of Polish life, the blessed otherness is again described as the true essence, this time by the young Karol Wojtyla, who would later become Pope John Paul II:

When your eyes are half-closed, space
fills again with substance beyond understanding—
the darkness of men is drawn back
cradling that goodness
which feeds you from each in the crowd
as long as you are silent

One of the paradoxes of higher consciousness is that the *"substance beyond understanding"* can be understood. It is beyond understanding in the sense that it is beyond the usual way of knowing and what is usually known. It is beyond the finite, the limited, the changeable, the mortal. But it can be sensed, and when it is sensed, life seems more vivid, more nourishing, more happy and more precious, imbued with Hopkins vision of *"the dearest freshness deep down things"* and *"the grandeur of God"*.

A great leap in consciousness takes place when a person matches the perception of the metaphysical essence of the outer world with the spiritual quality of one's own consciousness. Such insight is found in the poems of persons who practice meditation. In a flash of enlightenment, the Zen poet Bunan understands everything, including himself, to be one *"thingness"* at their most fundamental level and yet different things at their most expressed level. He writes:

The moon's the same old moon,
The flowers exactly as they were,
Yet I've become the thingness

Of all the things I see!

Because Bunan writes that *"the moon's the same old moon"*, we know that he hasn't lost his grip on reality; he has expanded it. As he appreciates a common unity between other things and himself, this can only make those things more dear to him.

Whether one comes to appreciate the essence of life by looking deeply within oneself or by looking deeply into the nature of things outside of oneself, one comes to the same confounding conclusion: What is most important is something that is in everything and everyone and yet greater than everything and everyone, a great commonality that when finally appreciated is not beyond you but your most enduring essence.

This flesh is but the visible out-pouring
Of a portentous and mighty thing,
Whereof each mortal knowing,
Becomes a king.[2]

The ancient Chinese sages knew the great commonality as the Way of things, the Tao. They concluded that this universal essence which is both unmanifest and manifest was not only an essence but also a process with organizing power. They understood it as a governing Way that co-ordinated all creation. In harmony with the natural Way, the Taoist found power and ease in living the life most natural for him. In the unfolding process of the essential Tao, the ancient poet T'ao Ch'ien found the *"deep meaning"* of life.

---

2. Excerpted from the poem *The Word* by Richard Realf.

T'AO CH'IEN
(China, 365-427)

I BUILT MY HUT

I built my hut in a zone of human habitation,
Yet near me there sounds no noise of horse or coach.
Would you know how that is possible?
A heart that is distant creates a wilderness round it.
I pluck chrysanthemums under the eastern hedge,
Then gaze long at the distant summer hills.
The mountain air is fresh at the dusk of day;
The flying birds two by two return.
In these things there lies a deep meaning;
Yet when we would express it, words suddenly fail us.

Translated by Arthur Waley

Notes

T'ao Ch'ien, born T'ao Yuan-ming, was a Taoist poet. He left a minor governmental post to settle in an agricultural village as a gentleman farmer. There he enjoyed a comfortable life, blessed with enough to eat and wine to drink and a wife and five sons. Because he was removed from the mainstream of political life, because his philosophy was Taoist and his poems admiring of the reclusive path, T'ao Ch'ien is considered a founder of the eremitic genre of Chinese poetry, even though a man with a wife and five children could hardly be considered a hermit.

Although he lived in a house *"in a zone of human habitation"*, T'ao Ch'ien was capable of a mental state of spiritual retreat akin to the religious hermits who dwelt in the wilderness of *"the distant summer hills"*. How was his mental retreat possible? *"A heart that is distant creates a wilderness round it."*

T'ao Ch'ien's poem seems as real to us today as it must have seemed sixteen hundred years ago. He describes a country gentleman's thoughtful pause in the garden around sunset. However, his simple, genuine description probably had more associations for his contemporaries than for us. For example, a season is often mentioned in Chinese poetry to set the tone for the poem, and T'ao Ch'ien has chosen *"summer"*, a time of sunny Yang energy and easy living, consistent with the Taoist philosophy of enjoying life without struggle. *"Chrysanthemums"* were prized not only as a flower but also as an herbal tea to promote health and longevity, valued by Taoists. The *"wilderness"* and *"mountain air"* were part of the habitat of the hermetic sages. The *"flying birds"* represented the freedom of the sky, and legend gave the wild geese (who are paired for life *"two by two"*) the status of messengers.

Their *"return"* represented the recurring continuity of the natural order of the Tao.

Yet, what is most important about this poem is the re-creation of a sensitive moment and the sense of *"deep meaning"* that is deeper and larger than human expression. This *"deep meaning"* is the Way—the way the birds return, the way the air is fresh, the way the chrysanthemums grow. It is the unspoken meaning of life. It is the Tao. Confronting its cosmic mystery, *"words suddenly fail us"*.

Because it is beyond evaluation, the permanent Tao is nameless; for convenience it is called Tao. It ranges from the void of the unseen, unmanifested non-being to the seen, manifested being which is the actualized potential of the unseen Tao. It is the essence that unites everything in one wholeness.

With a mind of emptiness, the Taoist enjoys an unobstructed accord with the governing Tao, so that everything seems to happen spontaneously in a self-so manner. The power of the Tao and the power of the sage are indistinguishable in the sage who lives his original nature in uncarved simplicity.

To return to his original nature, the Taoist seeks a rural life governed by the seasons and spared from the artificial values of civilization; he takes care of his health, and practices meditation and breathing exercises.

VICENTE HUIDOBRO
(Chile, 1893-1948)

IN

The heart of the bird
The heart that shines in the bird
The heart of the night
The night of the bird
The bird of the heart of the night

If the night should sing in the bird
In the bird forgotten in the sky
The sky lost in the night
I should say what there is in the heart
      that shines in the bird
The night lost in the sky
The sky lost in the bird
The bird lost in the oblivion of the bird
The night lost in the night
The sky lost in the sky

But the heart is the heart of the heart
And speaks with the mouth of the heart

Translated by H. R. Hays

Notes

This playful poem by one of South America's most famous poets pokes around at what is *"In"*, the inner essence. It is the essence of all the things in the poem: the bird, the heart, the night, the sky. Because it is the essence of all these things, they are interrelated, so that there can be *"the night of the bird . . . the bird of the night . . . the night lost in the sky . . . the sky lost in the night"* and so on as the poet explores many combinations. The essence that all these things have in common is the heart of consciousness, which can *"shine"* forth and *"sing"* and speak *"with the mouth of the heart"*. It is a universal consciousness which *"is in the heart that shines in the bird"* as its very being.

The poet plays with the idea of becoming *"lost"*. The heart of consciousness is so subtle that is easily lost to view and forgotten. But there is also another kind of *"lost"*, the oblivion of transcending. The poem's lulling, repetitious phrases lead the reader down a spiral of meaning which imitates the beginning of transcending.[3]

---

3. For an explanation of transcending, see the chapter on meditative experiences.

HILARY HUTTNER
(United States, 1951-)

THE HEART OF SECRETS

For someone who has time,
There is a secret in the way of things.

The paving stones soak up peace in sun,
And the heart feels a sweet silence.

The tree in the courtyard is green again,
And the heart knows life abiding.

The empty windows reflect the sky,
And the heart, so clear, reflects the truth.

The sky goes on without end.
The heart knows infinitude.

The clouds are majestic as the breath of God.
The heart sees the glory.

A shower of pollen dances in the sunshine,
And the heart leaps in bliss.

The statue sits beneath the tree, so still.
The heart rests in timelessness.

That round countenance, that mathematical smile!
The heart knows the heart of secrets.

Notes

This poem explores how the intuitive heart perceives the essence of ordinary things. The secret essence of each thing is perceived in turn as *"sweet silence ... life ... truth ... infinitude ... glory ... bliss ... timelessness"*. In the last verse, all these are known by the wise heart to be attributes of one mystery, *"the heart of secrets"*. The poem does not say what that heart is; if the poem did, it would not be a secret. But by now you know. The *"heart of secrets"* is the universal consciousness which is the essence of everything described in the poem.

The figure beneath the tree could be interpreted as a person sitting still as a statue in a meditative state, but the poet had in mind a garden statue of the Buddha. The round countenance connotes the fullness of contentment and wisdom. The mathematical curve of the smile evokes an association of the pure truth of mathematics.

DENISE LEVERTOV
(United States, 1923-)

THE BREATHING

An absolute
patience.
Trees stand
up to their knees in
fog. The fog
slowly flows
uphill.
       White
cobwebs, the grass
leaning where deer
have looked for apples.
The woods
from the brook to where
the top of the hill looks
over the fog, send up
not one bird.
So absolute, it is
no other than
happiness itself, a breathing
too quiet to hear.

Notes

The Breathing is a poem about the spiritual breath of life, about the hidden essence that is revealed in the private stillness of nature. In the undisturbed purity of the natural setting, the impression of fundamental nature is one of absoluteness, peace and abstract bliss.

The quality of absoluteness, enduring and imperturbable, is expressed in the *"absolute patience"*. The peacefulness of the scene is undisturbed by *"not one bird"*. The abstract bliss, *"so absolute, it is/ no other than/ happiness itself"* needs explanation:

To say that an essential ingredient of nature is something *"so absolute, it is no other than happiness itself"* may seem contrary to a scientific age struggling with material, environmental problems. However, such problems are disturbances on the surface level of life. Beneath the surface is an essence *"so absolute"* it is untouched by disturbances. It is unalloyed; it is *"no other than happiness itself"*. It is much like the metaphysical essence of Indian philosophy, *sat-chit-ananda*, in which sat means pure or absolute, chit means mind or consciousness, and ananda means cosmic bliss. It is the pure-bliss-consciousness which vibrates into life.

WALT WHITMAN
(United States, 1819-1892)

SONG OF MYSELF, 50

There is that in me—I do not know what it is—
     but I know it is in me.
Wrenched and sweaty—calm and cool then my body
     becomes,
I sleep—I sleep long.
I do not know it—it is without name—it is a word unsaid,
It is not in any dictionary, utterance, symbol.
Something it swings on more than the earth I swing on,
To it the creation is the friend whose embracing
     awakes me.
Perhaps I might tell more. Outlines! I plead for my
     brothers and sisters.
Do you see O my brothers and sisters?
It is not chaos or death—it is form, union, plan—
     it is eternal life—it is Happiness.

Whitman begins by saying honestly, *"There is that in me—I do not know what it is——"*. In the course of his poem, he works it out. After becoming *"calm"* and reflecting more on it, he senses, as he was wont to do, that it has a cosmic proportion matching the universe's vast *"creation"*. What is it that is in both Whitman and all of creation?

> *It is not chaos or death—it is form, union, plan—*
> *it is eternal life—it is Happiness.*

Whitman has hit upon the Essence. The first thing he describes is its organizing power. It is the opposite of *"chaos"*. It is *"form, union, plan"*. Next he mentions its unchanging, absolute quality, that it is *"eternal"*, and he immediately adds that it is *"life"*.

Then comes his proud discovery: it is Happiness with a capital H. This is not a personal happiness but a universal attribute in which the individual participates. Sensing it within himself, *"in me"*, Whitman comes to the same conclusion that Denise Levertov comes to generations later when she senses the essence in the landscape before her. Their conclusions are the same because what they are both sensing is the same, eternal, universal essence, pervading the outer world and the inner mind.

DENISE LEVERTOV
(United States, 1923-)

CITY PSALM

The killings continue, each second
pain and misfortune extend themselves
in the genetic chain, injustice is done knowingly,
    and the air
bears the dust of decayed hopes,
yet breathing those fumes, walking the thronged
pavements among crippled lives, jackhammers
raging, a parking lot painfully agleam
in the May sun, I have seen
not behind but within, within the
dull grief, blown grit, hideous
concrete façades, another grief, a gleam
as of dew, an abode of mercy,
have heard not behind but within noise
a humming that drifted into a quiet smile.
Nothing was changed, all was revealed otherwise;
not that horror was not, not that the killings
    did not continue,
not that I thought there was to be no more despair,
but that as if transparent all disclosed
an otherness that was blesséd, that was bliss.
I saw Paradise in the dust of the street.

Notes

    Anyone who has lived in New York City, as the poet
did, will sympathize 100% with the harsh realities described in this poem. The *"fumes"*, *"thronged pavements"*,

and *"jackhammers"* are peculiarly New York; the other, far greater miseries are all too common. Ms. Levertov's description of bliss is all the more believable because she does not deny the horror of the ordinary world.

It is to the poet's credit that she is able is perceive an absolute *"bliss"* existing in paradox with the daily misery of urban life. Many people can sense bliss in a glorious natural setting or in the refuge of meditation, but only a developed person has the flexibility to appreciate simultaneously both extremes of existence: the subtle bliss and the gross sensations of life in its most active turmoil.

The poet says that she has seen *"within"* the grit and heard *"within"* the noise, meaning by *"within"* that she has sensed the inner essence. She finds that essence within to have a spiritual upliftment, *"a gleam"* and *"an abode of mercy"*. *"Within noise"* she senses an inner vibration, a subtle *"humming"*. The humming has the quality of bliss, revealed when it *"drifted into a quiet smile"*; conversely the bliss has the quality of humming, of vibration.

Her description of mystical perception is classic: *"Nothing was changed, all was revealed otherwise. . . as if transparent all disclosed/ an otherness that was blessèd, that was bliss"*. When you have a flash of higher consciousness, the objects in sight continue to have the same shape and color, but added to that sight is a new level of apprehending what you are seeing. The objects seem less material, as something which is *"transparent"* seems less material and is capable of revealing what was hidden before. What the objects reveal is *"blessed"* and *"bliss"*.

Ms. Levertov does not treat bliss as a human feeling but as a metaphysical essence, a reality that she could see rather than a mood to be felt. When she uses italics in the last line of her poem, she means to emphasize that she truly did see it: *"I saw Paradise in the dust of the street."*

KAROL WOJTYLA, POPE JOHN PAUL II
(Poland, 1920-)

WHEN YOU OPEN YOUR EYES
DEEP IN A WAVE

Transparent after fresh rain, the stones glisten
as each passing step touches them slightly.
Soon it will be evening. Banging. Doors open.
How many people will enter? How many will
thaw in the light from the windows?
Evening has come. Now and again the face
of a passerby opens the human wall—then
window lights carry it over
to some other place nearby.
The wall now contracts, now widens; still the same.
Eyes can break out of the dark, only just—
the wall is easy.

But, I tell you, your sight alone
scarcely catches people as they flow
on the wave of florescent lights.
They are revealed by what is most concealed
within them, that which no flame
will burn out.

When your eyes are half-closed, space
fills again with substance beyond understanding—
the darkness of men is drawn back
cradling that goodness
which feeds you from each in the crowd
as long as you are silent,
which your shouts
turn to dust.

No, no it is not simply you, each of you,
and were it so,
your presence not only exists, it reveals.

And yet—if eyes could only be opened
not from habit, but differently;
then, then not to forget
their vision filled with delight.

Translated by Jerzey Peterkiewicz

Notes

The title of this poem is so apt that it captures the theme our book. *"When you open your eyes"* is a way of saying when you perceive with a new, awakened consciousness. *"Deep in a wave"* means on a deep level of awareness. The *"wave"* is an image of thought in the mind, just as the *"shores"* are a mental plane in Wojtyla's other poem *Shores of Silence.*

What the poet sees when he opens to a deep level of awareness is the *"substance beyond understanding"*. He has some important things to say about its presence: It is *"most concealed"*; it is everlasting, *"that which no flame will burn out"*; it is revealed when *"the darkness of men is drawn back"*; it is *"goodness"*; it is nourishing to your own spirit as it *"feeds you from each in the crowd"*; and you can perceive it *"as long as you are silent"*.

The *"substance"* seen with the altered sight of *"eyes half-closed"* by which *"space fills again with substance beyond understanding"* is a sea of divine intelligence that fills space and all things with the non-material, all-permeating filling of spirit. As spirit, it transcends mortal life. Thus the poet suggests that it is beyond ordinary understanding.

Yet because the spiritual substance is also part of yourself, it can be recognized. *"When you open your eyes deep in a wave"*, at a deep level in the sea of your own consciousness, you become familiar with the sea of consciousness and you have a glimpse of its unboundedness. When you sense it subtly around you, in other people, it strengthens you; it is *"that goodness which feeds you"*.

Because this *"most concealed"* essence exists on the most silent level of being, the poet suggests that the experience will last *"as long as you are silent"*. Here he refers to interior silence, a psycho-physiological state which also appears in his poem *Shores of Silence*. When this inner silence is combined with a waking-state activity, an expanded waking-state results.   Then eyes are opened *"differently"*, in a more enlightened state of consciousness, *"their vision filled with delight"*.

GERARD MANLEY HOPKINS
(England, 1844-1889)

GOD'S GRANDEUR

The world is charged with the grandeur of God.
  It will flame out, like shining from shook foil;
  It gathers to a greatness, like the ooze of oil
Crushed. Why do men then now not reck his rod?
Generations have trod, have trod, have trod;
    And all is seared with trade; bleared, smeared
      with toil;
And wears man's smudge and shares man's smell:
      the soil
Is bare now, nor can foot feel, being shod.

And for all this, nature is never spent;
  There lives the dearest freshness deep down things;
And though the last lights off the black West went
  Oh, morning, at the brown brink eastward,
      springs—
Because the Holy Ghost over the bent
World broods with warm breast and with ah!
      bright wings.

Notes

Gerard Manley Hopkins was a Jesuit priest, and his poetry reflects his religious beliefs. He calls the essence *"the grandeur of God"*. He describes a glimpse of its glory as a sparkle that is momentarily here and there, *"like shining from shook foil"*.

He next compares the essence to an *"oil"* that oozes out when the seed is crushed, showing that the oil was a hidden essence permeating the seed.

Yet there is a great discrepancy in the co-existence of the divine and the mundane—for the world that is *"charged with the grandeur of God"* is also *"smeared with toil;/ And wears man's smudge"*.

Overcoming the distance between the divine and the mundane is the spirit of the *"Holy Ghost"* and the touch of immortal intelligence in nature, so that *"nature is never spent"* and *"There lives the dearest freshness deep down things"*.

BUNAN
(Japan, 1602-1676)

UNTITLED

The moon's the same old moon,
The flowers exactly as they were,
Yet I've become the thingness
Of all the things I see!

Translated by Lucien Stryk and Takashi Ikemoto

Notes

In this short poem, Bunan puts his finger on a key point. He understands himself in terms of an essence; *"thingness"* is how it is translated. This thingness is the suchness of things, the beingness, the presence. It is consciousness itself, not as an individual's awareness, but consciousness as an essence, as a field of being, as the great commonality, as the abstract value which goes along with every concrete thing.

Although it is in things, the thingness is not material. Because it is nonmaterial, it is not limited to material boundaries. It is found within the subjective mind as well as in the objective world. So it is not surprising that Bunan observes the same thingness within and without. His observation is similar to the realization of Joho, who declared in his poem on awakening, *"It's everywhere!"*

Bunan emphasizes that despite his great discovery about the common essence of things and himself, things like the moon and flowers are still *"exactly as they were"*. Like recognizing a face in a crowd, the same face that was a stranger is found to be a friend.

The commonality that Bunan apprehends is closer than a friend; it is himself, his cosmic Self. His universal Self is the essence, *"the thingness of all the things I see"* which he becomes when he recognizes it. This self-realization is a perception of unity consciousness, the state of awareness that unites all things within the Self.

RICHARD REALF
(United States 1834-1878)

THE WORD

O Earth! Thou hast not any wind that blows
Which is not music; every weed of thine
Pressed rightly flows in aromatic wine;
And humble hedge-row flower that grows,

And every little brown bird that doth sing,
Hath something greater than itself, and bears
A living word to every living thing,
Albeit holds the message unawares.

All shapes and sounds have something which is not
Of them: a spirit broods amid the grass;
Vague outlines of the Everlasting Thought
Lie in the melting shadows as they pass;

The touch of an eternal presence thrills
The fringes of the sunsets and the hills.
While soul within its prison speaks to soul,
Hailing the habitation as the whole!

This flesh is but the visible out-pouring
Of a portentous and mighty thing,
Whereof each mortal knowing,
Becomes a king.

Notes

The *"Word"* in this poem is the *"Everlasting Thought"* indwelling the whole of creation. It is cosmic intelligence and cosmic knowledge. The humblest weed is exalted by this divine *"spirit"* which is a glorious *"eternal presence"*.

To consider this intellectually is one thing, but to experience it is another. It is possible for the senses to take in the sublime quality in a scene of nature as an aesthetic experience without the intellect understanding why. People sense the divine intelligence in nature, but not knowing what they sense, they call it the beauty of nature.

This poem makes nine metaphysical assertions about the essence of existence: 1) There is a *"spirit"*. 2) The spirit is an *"eternal presence"*. 3) The presence has the quality of *"thought"*. 4) It is in *"all shapes and sounds"* and *"every living thing"*. 5) The presence makes of them one *"whole"*. 6) It is *"portentous and mighty"*. 7) The presence imparts to each thing *"something greater than itself"*. 8) By knowing this, a person becomes *"a king"*. 9) The perception of the presence is as delightful as *"music"* or *"aromatic wine"*.

The poem concludes with quite a claim: that by knowing the secret of the indwelling Everlasting Thought, *"each mortal knowing becomes a king"*. The mortal person becomes a king when he experiences the sublime because the *"portentous and mighty"* presence imparts to each person and thing *"something greater than itself"* and because it governs the creation as a *"whole"*. However, there is more to *"knowing"* than just reading this poem. How one arrives at such a state of knowing and how one perceives and thinks from the level of the *"Word"* so as to become *"a king"* is a challenge to be answered by the human potential movements.

List of Poems in Chapter Seven

The Heart of Herakles
by Kenneth Rexroth

On the Beach at Night Alone
by Walt Whitman

Over All Presides the Universal Soul
by Plotinus

All Are But Parts
by Alexander Pope

Renascence
by Edna St. Vincent Millay

Many Truly
by Hugo Von Hofmannsthal

The Elusive Ones
by Rumi

I Saw One Life, and Felt that It Was Joy
by William Wordsworth

7

UNITY

At the heart of mysticism is the consciousness of the One. It is the first principle listed by the philosopher W. T. Stace and his colleagues in their cross-cultural definition of mysticism in the world's religions. They agreed on seven points:[1]

1. There is a unifying vision, in which the One is perceived by the senses in and through many objects, so that all is One.
2. The One is apprehended as an inner life or presence in all things, so that nothing is really dead.
3. This brings a sense of reality, which is objective and true.
4. There is a feeling of satisfaction, joy and bliss.
5. There is a feeling of the holy and sacred, which is the specifically religious element of the experience.
6. There is a feeling that it is paradoxical.
7. There is a feeling that it is inexpressible in words.

The One has the quality of consciousness. Consciousness includes existence, intelligence, awareness, order and creativity. Human beings, too, have consciousness. At a fundamental level, the omnipresent consciousness of the One and the individual consciousness of the human being have a common ground. When human awareness expands to appreciate the underlying field of the universal consciousness of the One, a person experiences a new quality of awareness, unity consciousness.

---

1. Geoffrey Parrinder, *Mysticism in the World's Religions* (New York: Oxford University Press, 1976), p. 11.

In the last chapter, we listened to poets who perceived the One to be an indwelling presence that was the essence of all things, animate and inanimate. Now we hear the testimony of poets who have perceived the world as One, not merely from the perspective of a finite observer, but from the infinite perspective of unity consciousness. They have perceived the world from the perspective of that common, unifying field of Wholeness which makes the universe one life.

Kenneth Rexroth described it on a summer night beneath the stars. He seemed to fall into a meditative state, a state of restful alertness in which his body was very still but his eyes were open and his mind was alert. In that stillness, the limits of his body receded from his awareness, and his own existence was no longer delimited from the existence of the stars that he was observing. He wrote:

The stars stand around me
Like gold eyes. I can no longer
Tell where I begin and leave off.
The faint breeze in the dark pines,
And the invisible grass,
The tipping earth, the swarming stars
Have an eye that sees itself.

Rexroth is but one of generations of American poets who have written of transcendence, essence and unity. Emerson and Whitman, the nineteenth century transcendental poets, gave American poetry a mysticism which has been popular ever since. It is as good a starting point as any to say that the New Age began in America when Emerson read the Hindu *Bhagavad Gita* and the Neoplatonic *Enneads* of Plotinus. Emerson became the first literary giant to admire Whitman. Whitman seemed to echo Emerson's essays when he wrote in his poem *On the Beach at Night Alone*: *"A vast similitude interlocks all"*.

The mystery of the unity of all things has drawn together philosophy and physics. The physicist David Bohm has proposed that *"relativity and quantum theory. . . both imply the need to look on the universe as an undivided whole, in which all parts of the universe, including the observer and his instruments, merge and unite in one totality. . . . This new form of insight can perhaps best be called Undivided Wholeness in Flowing Movement."*[2]

Another physicist, John Hagelin, has combined modern physics and a revival of ancient Indian theories. He proposes that fundamental to everything is a field of all possibilities which unifies everything manifesting therefrom, a unified field which is pure consciousness and which can account for the field effects of human consciousness as well as quantum events.[3]

Katherin Hayles has summed up the new appreciation for unity very well:

"The twentieth century has seen a profound transformation in the ground of its thought, a change catalyzed and validated by relativity theory, quantum mechanics, and particle physics. But the shift in perspective is by no means confined to physics; analogous developments have occurred in a number of disciplines, among them philosophy, linguistics, mathematics, and literature. . . . I shall speak of it as a revolution in world view. . . . Characteristic models are a cosmic dance, a network of events, and an energy field. A dance, a network, a field—the phrases imply a reality that has no detachable parts, indeed no enduring, unchanging parts at all. Composed not of particles but of events, it is in constant motion, ren-

2. David Bohm, *Wholeness and the Implicate Order* (London: Ark, 1987), p. 11.
3. John Hagelin, "Is Consciousness the Unified Field?" *Modern Science and Vedic Science,* 1:1 (1987).

particles but of events, it is in constant motion, ren-
dered dynamic by interactions that are simultaneously
affecting each other. As the dance metaphor implies,
its harmonious, rhythmic patterns of motion include
the observer as an integral participant. Its distin-
guishing characteristics then are its fluid, dynamic
nature, the inclusion of the observer, the absence of
detachable parts, and the mutuality of component
interactions. "[4]

The sense of unity is also with us today in the ecology movement, which views our planet as united in one ecology. The ancients knew this and more. Plotinus taught that *"the universe is one living organism"*[5] and that *"Over all presides the Universal Soul"*.[6] Similarly, the unity of nature was understood in pre-industrial England, when Alexander Pope wrote:

All are but parts of one stupendous whole,
Whose body Nature is, and God the soul;

Human beings are part of this same *"stupendous whole"*. When people become conscious of this wholeness, they may have experiences such as these: 1) a sense of the universe as an inseparable wholeness, 2) a sympathetic connection to other lives so that all are felt as part of one life, 3) a paradoxical sense of one's self in inanimate things and in the processes of nature, making them seem delightfully dear and an expression of one's self, 4) a switch in the emphasis of one's attention from the foreground of different forms to the background of the universal essence or

4. N. Katherine Hayles, *The Cosmic Web* (Ithaca: Cornell University Press, 1984), p. 15.
5. Ennead III.ii.8, as found in Grace Turnbull, *The Essence of Plotinus* (New York: Oxford University Press, 1948), p. 80.
6. Ennead VI.viii, as found in Charles Albertson, *Lyra Mystica* (New York: Macmillan, 1932), pp. 12-13.

field that they have in common, 5) an impression that everything is made of consciousness or spirit, 6) a re-evaluation of one's self to identify with the Whole 7) feelings of harmony, invulnerability, peace, bliss, appreciation of beauty, creativity, unconditional love and intuition that seem associated with the grand scale of the Whole.

Experiences like these leap off the pages of Edna St. Vincent Millay's startling poem *Renascence*:

I screamed, and—Lo!—Infinity
Came down and settled over me;
     *   *   *
Until it seemed I must behold
Immensity made manifold;
     *   *   *
I saw and heard, and knew at last
The How and Why of all things, past,
And present, and forevermore.
     *   *   *
No hurt I did not feel, no death
That was not mine; mine each last breath
     *   *   *
Mine, pity like the pity of God.
     *   *   *
And, through and over everything,
A sense of glad awakening.
     *   *   *
O God, I cried, no dark disguise
Can e'er hereafter hide from me
Thy radiant identity!

A sympathetic connection with all other human lives in the greater destiny of the whole is the theme of Hugo Von Hofmannsthal's poem *Many Truly*. His sympathetic connection leads to his social concern for the welfare of other people.

I can never cast off from my eyelids
Lassitudes of long-forgotten peoples,
Nor from my astounded soul can banish
Soundless falls of stars through outer distances.

Many destinies with mine are woven;
Being plays them all through one another,
And my part is larger than this slender
Life's ascending flame or narrow lyre.

From the perspective of unity, all human beings, indeed all life and all forms, are part of one undying life and one formless form. Rumi's poem *The Elusive Ones* about the union of opposites can only be understood from the perspective of unity. In unity, *"Good and evil, dead and alive, everything blooms from one natural stem."* Because that *"one natural stem"* is supporting all of existence, *"Any direction you turn, it's one vision."* It is the vision of the One, which is the fundamental consciousness and being of all, which is both a metaphysical field and an identity, the great, common existence which makes differences seem humorous by comparison.

Wordsworth described it most eloquently. He felt *"the sentiment of Being spread/ O'er all"*. He *"saw one life, and felt that it was joy"*. He saw a reality that the ancient yogis called *sat-chit-ananda*, absolute-consciousness-bliss. It is an insight into both the unity of existence and the blissful nature of the universal consciousness.

If only it were more common for human consciousness to be anchored in the vision of universal consciousness, then exploitation and fear would subside because all would be appreciated in terms of one Self. Plotinus wished for this in ancient times:[7]

---

7. Ennead VI.v.1, as found in Grace Turnbull, *The Essence of Plotinus* (New York: Oxford University Press, 1948), p. 188.

"All men instinctively affirm the God in each of us to be one, the same in all. Were this really effective in their thought, men would be at rest, finding their stay in that oneness and identity, so that nothing could wrench them from this unity."

KENNETH REXROTH
(United States, 1905-1982)

THE HEART OF HERAKLES

Lying under the stars,
In the summer night,
Late, while the autumn
Constellations climb the sky,
As the Cluster of Hercules
Falls down the west,
I put the telescope by
And watch Deneb
Move towards the zenith.
My body is asleep. Only
My eyes and brain are awake.
The stars stand around me
Like gold eyes. I can no longer
Tell where I begin and leave off.
The faint breeze in the dark pines,
And the invisible grass,
The tipping earth, the swarming stars
Have an eye that sees itself.

from The Lights in the Sky are Stars

Notes

Rexroth describes some interesting physiological details. With his body as still as though *"asleep"* but with his eyes and brain *"awake"*, he is in a state of restful alertness similar to the restful alertness of meditation. However, instead of his senses being directed inwards for meditation, his senses are directed outward to observe the wide constellations of the night sky.

The next detail is a turning point for him. He finds, *"I can no longer/ Tell where I begin and leave off."* In a state of restful alertness, he has lost the sensation of his body, as in sleep, and so he does not physically feel the boundaries of his body. But this experience has more than a physical significance. It prepares him for a new notion of himself, a self that is not fenced off from the universe around him. Quite naturally, he has come upon the same phenomenon that Plotinus suggested to his metaphysical students: To appreciate the universal unity, think of yourself without boundaries.

Now the observer and the observed become one. The gazing eyes of Rexroth are a pair of eyes of the wholeness *"that sees itself"*.

WALT WHITMAN
(United States, 1819-1892)

ON THE BEACH AT NIGHT ALONE

On the beach at night alone,
As the old mother sways her to and fro
    singing her husky song,
As I watch the bright stars shining, I think a thought
    of the clef of the universes and of the future.

A vast similitude interlocks all,
All spheres, grown, ungrown, small, large, suns,
    moon, planets,
All distances of time, all inanimate forms,
All souls, all living bodies, though they be
    ever so different or in different worlds,
All gaseous, watery, vegetable, mineral processes,
    the fishes, the brutes,
All nations, colors, barbarisms, civilizations,
    languages,
All identities that have existed or may exist on this
    globe, any globe,
All lives and deaths, all of the past, present, future,
This vast similitude spans them, and always has
    spann'd,
And shall forever span them and compactly hold and
    enclose them.

Notes

Whitman begins with a scene of solitude on the beach. *"The old mother"* is the swaying ocean, lapping on the shore with *"a husky song"*. Looking up at the expanse of stars, he has an insight into the universal nature of life, *"a thought of the clef of the universes . . ."*

He realizes that *"a vast similitude interlocks all"*. Quickly he begins to calculate what that includes—all planets, all time, all inanimate forms, all souls, all life, even extraterrestrial identities from different globes! Moreover, he realizes that it has always been this way, that the *"vast similitude"* has always spanned and encompassed and held into one wholeness everything in the universe.

The perception of the unity of the universe is the natural result of an expansive awareness. As awareness expands, there is a sense of being more awake, of taking in more and understanding more of its spiritual value. Whitman knew that he had entered a higher state of consciousness, though he did not use that term. He simply wrote: *"I cannot be awake, for nothing looks to me as it did before,/ Or else I am awake for the first time, and all before has been a mean sleep."*[8]

---

8. Justin Kaplan, *Walt Whitman, A Life* (New York: Simon & Schuster, 1980), p. 17. Quoting a fragment of Whitman's jottings.

PLOTINUS
(Roman Empire, in Greek, 205-270)

OVER ALL PRESIDES THE UNIVERSAL SOUL

Over all presides the Universal Soul.
Created things are born and die.
The Universal Soul is Being, pure,
Ageless life which changes not.
To contemplate this Soul
We must be worthy by nobility;
We must release our minds from error,
Immerse ourselves in meditation,
Withdraw our thoughts from things that fascinate
    the eye,
Subdue the agitations of the flesh,
Silence the tumult of the earth and air,
And let our souls stand in the presence of the Power
Which from all sides overflows the world,
Which penetrates it intimately, lights it up
Even as the sun irradiates the darkness of a cloud.
Thus the Universal Soul, descending,
Redeems the world from death,
Imparting movement, life and immortality.
It is the Soul that holds the world, immense and
    manifold,
Within the bonds of universal unity.

Translated and adapted by
Kenneth Guthrie and Charles Albertson
from Ennead VI.viii

Notes

Plotinus was a cosmopolitan citizen of the Roman Empire. Born in Egypt and educated in Greek culture according to the fashion of the day, he was steeped in the wisdom of Plato and other Greek philosophers. Having drunk his fill in Alexandria, Egypt, a mecca of higher learning in the ancient world, he searched abroad for adventure and the mysticism of Persia and India. Maturing in his own wisdom, Plotinus synthesized in Rome a metaphysical philosophy whose power made him the progenitor of mysticism in the Western world. His mystical ideas leapt from the Pagan world to Christendom through his influence on St. Augustine, passed on through generations of Europeans versed in Greek and Latin, and entered the stream of American thought through Emerson's admiration of his philosophy. To Plotinus can be traced the Neoplatonic root of the lineage of the New Age.

Hailed as the re-incarnation of Plato, Plotinus was a philosopher and a teacher but not a poet. His *Enneads* were lectures written down in an elliptical Greek style and then edited by his disciple Porphyry. A modern translator and editor have worked some excerpts into verses that reveal the beauty of the wisdom of Plotinus.

The opening premise of the passage presented here is that *"Over all presides the Universal Soul"*. For Plotinus, the Universal Soul is contained in the Divine Mind which in turn is contained in the One, which he also calls Unity, the First, Principle, the Good, the All, the All-Transcending, Primarily Existent, Self-Existent, the Supreme, the Maker. In his vision, there is a transcendent Primarily Existent and then an extension of that Light radiating as Divine Mind and Universal Soul. The Universal Soul indwells humankind, imparting universal Life to individual life and immortality to the human soul.

Thus the Universal Soul, descending,
Redeems the world from death,
Imparting movement, life and immortality.
It is the Soul that holds the world, immense and
        manifold,
Within the bonds of universal unity.

Plotinus ties together the existence of the Universal Soul, the individual's contemplation of it, the *"power"* of that relationship, and the *"universal unity"* that is the inevitable result of the existence of the Universal Soul.

To know the Universal Soul, Plotinus recommends meditation. Though easier said than done, he advocates releasing the mind from ignorance, withdrawing the senses from outer sensory experience, subduing the needs of the flesh and entering into a state of silence. How to release, withdraw, subdue and become silent? In Ennead V.iii.17, Plotinus gives the answer: *"Let all else go!"*[9]

In other passages, Plotinus gives more advice for the seeker who attempts to know the Supreme through contemplation. In Ennead V.iii.8 he suggests, *"Think of the traces of this Light upon the soul, then say to yourself that such and more beautiful and broader and more radiant is the Light Itself . . . Thus we lead our own soul up to the Divine, so that it holds itself an image of that Being, its life becoming an imprint and likeness of the Highest . . ."*[10] He elaborates in Ennead V.viii.10-11, *"we must bring the vision within and see it as one with ourselves. . . . The novice must hold himself constantly under some image of the Divine Being . . . and . . . be no longer the seer, but as that place has made him, the seen. To see the Divine as*

---

9. Grace Turnbull, *The Essence of Plotinus* (New York: Oxford University Press, 1948), p. 163.   10. *Ibid.*, p. 161.

something external is to be outside of It; to become It is to be most truly in Beauty. "[11]

The resulting illumination is reminiscent of yogis:

> *In our self-seeing, there is a communion with the self restored to its purity. . . . For in this seeing, we neither see nor distinguish nor are there two. The man is changed, no longer himself nor self-belonging; he is merged with the Supreme, sunken into It, one with It; only in separation is there duality. This is why the vision baffles telling; for how could a man bring back tidings of the Supreme as detached when he has seen It as one with himself? . . . Since beholder was one with beheld, and it was not a vision compassed but a unity apprehended, the man formed by this mingling with the Supreme would, if he but remembered, carry Its image impressed upon him. He is become the Unity, having no diversity either in relation to himself or anything else; no movement, no passion, no out-looking desire, once this ascent is achieved. Reason is in abeyance and intellection and even the very self; caught away, God-possessed, in perfect stillness. All the being calmed, he turns neither to this side nor to that, nor even inwards to himself; utterly resting, he has become rest itself. . . . [He is] like one who, having penetrated the inner sanctuary, leaves the temple images behind; for there his conversing is not with image, not with trace, but with Deity himself . . .*
>
> *There is thus a converse in virtue of which the essential man outgrows Being, becomes identical with the Transcendent of Being. He that knows himself to be one with This, has in himself the likeness of the Supreme . . .* "[12]

---

11. *Ibid.*, p. 177.   12. *Ibid.*, pp. 221-222.

ALEXANDER POPE
(England, 1688-1744)

ALL ARE BUT PARTS

All are but parts of one stupendous whole,
Whose body Nature is, and God the soul;
That, changed through all, and yet in all the same,
Great in the earth, as in th'ethereal frame,
Warms in the sun, refreshes in the breeze,
Glows in the stars and blossoms in the trees,
Lives through all life, extends through all extent,
Spreads undivided, operates unspent:
Breathes in our soul, informs our mortal part;
As full, as perfect, in a hair as heart;
As full, as perfect, in vile man that mourns
As the rapt Seraphim, that sings and burns:
To him, no high, no low, no great, no small—
He fills, he bounds, connects and equals all...
All nature is but art unknown to thee:
All chance, direction which thou canst not see:
All discord, harmony not understood;
All partial evil, universal good.

Pope's talent for epigram is wonderfully applied in this poem. In a single rhyme, he sums up the perennial wisdom of the mystics:

All are but parts of one stupendous whole,
Whose body Nature is, and God the soul;

He addresses the paradox of the enlightened vision, that simultaneously the One is appreciated as the self-same in all the variety of creation, *"changed through all, and yet in all the same"*. It is something *"perfect"* lending a precious value to mortal and angel, small and great alike, making them *"equals all"* and connecting them.

Pope also describes another key point of mystical experience: a sense of intelligent arrangement. In a mystical appreciation of God and God's creation, one sees an intelligence where the world had seemed soulless before, as though a stuffed animal had come to life. One sees in the beauty of nature a divine engineering and an artful arrangement which makes it seem even more beautiful. One sees in the dance of life a *"direction"* and *"harmony"* that leads to *"good"* in the end.

EDNA ST. VINCENT MILLAY
(United States, 1892-1950)

RENASCENCE[13]

All I could see from where I stood
Was three long mountains and a wood;
I turned and looked another way,
And saw three islands in a bay.

           *   *   *

And all at once things seemed so small
My breath came short, and scarce at all.

           *   *   *

I screamed, and——Lo!——Infinity
Came down and settled over me;
Forced back my scream into my chest;
Bent back by arm upon my breast;
And, pressing of the Undefined
The definition on my mind,
Held up before my eyes a glass
Through which my shrinking sight did pass
Until it seemed I must behold
Immensity made manifold;
Whispered to me a word whose sound
Deafened the air for worlds around,
And brought unmuffled to my ears

---

13. *Renascence* is a long poem of 214 lines. Asterisks indicate where stanzas or the opening lines of a stanza have been omitted, and an ellipsis (. . .) indicates where the remainder of a stanza was omitted.

The gossiping of friendly spheres,
The creaking of the tented sky,
The ticking of Eternity.

I saw and heard, and knew at last
The How and Why of all things, past,
And present, and forevermore.
The Universe, cleft to the core,
Lay open to my probing sense . . .
For my omniscience paid I toll
In infinite remorse of soul.

All sin was of my sinning, all
Atoning mine, and mine the gall
Of all regret. Mine was the weight
Of every brooded wrong, the hate
That stood behind each envious thrust,
Mine every greed, mine every lust.

*   *   *

No hurt I did not feel, no death
That was not mine; mine each last breath
That, crying, met an answering cry
From the compassion that was I.
All suffering mine, and mine its rod;
Mine, pity like the pity of God.

*   *   *

Long had I lain thus, craving death . . .

*   *   *

And all at once, and over all

The pitying rain began to fall;

*   *   *

I would I were alive again
To kiss the fingers of the rain . . .

*   *   *

Oh God, I cried, give me new birth,
And put me back upon the earth! . . .

I ceased; and through the breathless hush
That answered me, the far-off rush
Of herald wings came whispering
Like music down the vibrant string
Of my ascending prayer . . .

I know not how such things can be;
I only know there came to me
A fragrance such as never clings
To aught save happy living things;
A sound as of some joyous elf
Singing sweet songs to please himself,
And, through and over everything,
A sense of glad awakening. . . .

Ah! Up then from the ground sprang I
And hailed the Earth with such a cry
As is not heard save from a man
Who has been dead, and lives again.
About the trees my arms I wound;
Like one gone mad I hugged the ground;
I raised my quivering arms on high;
I laughed and laughed into the sky;

Till at my throat a strangling sob
Caught fiercely, and a great heart-throb
Sent instant tears into my eyes:
O God, I cried, no dark disguise
Can e'er hereafter hide from me
Thy radiant identity!

Thou canst not move across the grass
But my quick eyes will see Thee pass,
Nor speak, however silently,
But my hushed voice will answer Thee.
I know the path that tells Thy way
Through the cool eve of the day;
God, I can push the grass apart
And lay my finger on Thy heart!

The world stands out on either side
No wider than the heart is wide;
Above the world is stretched the sky,—
No higher than the soul is high.
The heart can push the sea and land
Farther away on either hand;
The soul can split the sky in two,
And let the face of God shine through.
But East and West will pinch the heart
That can not keep them pushed apart;
And he whose soul is flat — the sky
Will cave in on him by and by.

Notes

Renascence was the first poem published by Edna St. Vincent Millay. Its success launched her career as a poet.

The title *"Renascence"*, meaning re-birth, reflects the plot of the poem, in which the poet has an overwhelming vision, longs for relief in death, then longs for life and is revived into a new state of appreciation of the world and God. The excerpts presented here focus on the poet's cosmic vision and on her new state of appreciation.

The vision is preceded by a physiological change, a reduction in breath. A reduction or suspension of breath often accompanies a transition to a spiritual state of awareness because when the usual activity of the body is stilled, a subtler style of functioning and perceiving is made possible which goes beyond the limitations of the individual. A sudden shift into a state beyond the usual boundaries, a state the poet calls *"Infinity"*, makes the ordinary activity of shouting in surprise a struggle in the opposite direction, and thus Millay reports *"Infinity . . . Forced back my scream"*.

The *"pressing of the Undefined"* is another way of describing the transcendent state beyond boundaries. It seems difficult to bear for the poet because it comes as a shock, rather than as something prepared by spiritual practice. She stretches to comprehend the *"Immensity made manifold"*.

She hears *"a word whose sound/ Deafened the air for worlds around"*. Could she have heard the cosmic Om, the vibration of creation heard by yogis? She becomes privy to the functioning of nature, extending in space as far as the distant *"spheres"* and in time through *"Eternity"*. She is at the level of all knowledge, where she finds *"The How and Why of all things, past,/ And present, and forevermore"*.

Her vision has changed her perspective from that of an individual human being to that of the Wholeness of which everything, including herself, is a part. From that perspective, she has access to the knowledge of all the *"manifold"* parts of the *"Immensity"* of the Wholeness. She enjoys *"omniscience"*. But because she is not established in the transcendent bliss which is beyond alteration, she is about to be overwhelmed by a shift in focus to the suffering of the changing world.

Aware of the totality, she becomes aware of all *"sin"*, all *"hurt"*, all *"death"*, and all the human emotion associated with them. Fortunately, she responds as personages with a consciousness of the totality classically respond, with divine *"compassion"*.

Her visionary experience is too much for her to bear. She longs for *"death"*, but nature has compassion on her. The *"pitying rain"* revives her desire to live. Quickly her desire is fulfilled.

Not only is she revived, but her senses are glorified with the perception of divine bliss. As she awakens, she hears the celestial *"rush"* of heralding angels and the vibration of her own prayer, she smells a glorious *"fragrance"*, and she hears a joyous *"sound"*. She has *"a sense of glad awakening"*, and her bliss is uncontainable as she laughs and laughs. She has come back from a taste of the Infinite's comprehension of the totality. Now she has a new appreciation of the Infinite in her familiar world. Her heart throbs with a divine appreciation that moves her to tears. Everywhere she sees the *"radiant identity"* of God.

MANY TRULY

Many truly down below must perish
Where the heavy oars of ships are passing;
Others by the helm may have their dwelling,
Knowing flights of birds and starry countries.

Many lie with heavy limbs, remaining
Near the roots of life obscurely tangled.
Certain chairs to others are appointed,
Near to sibyls, queens for their companions.
There they sit as though at home, made easy,
Easy in their heads, in their hands easy.

Yet from their existence falls a shadow
Reaching the existence of those others,
And the easy are to the burdened
Bound, as to earth and air, by living.

I can never cast off from my eyelids
Lassitudes of long-forgotten peoples,
Nor from my astounded soul can banish
Soundless falls of stars through outer distances.

Many destinies with mine are woven;
Being plays them all through one another,
And my part is larger than this slender
Life's ascending flame or narrow lyre.

Translated by Vernon Watkins

Notes

The recognition of the unity of life leads to a social consciousness that we are all in this together. Whether one's station in life is as lowly as an ancient oarsman's or as commanding as a helmsman's, all lives are *"bound"* together on that subtle level of *"living"*.

On the level of unity which extends throughout time and space, the *"lassitudes of long-forgotten peoples"* are part of the whole, as much as the most distant *"stars"*. The stress of all living things and all events has an impact on every human being, even when people are not conscious of that collective effect. The poet is conscious of it. He is conscious, too, that he plays a reciprocal role, *"larger"* than his *"life's"* individual *"flame"* or the Apollonian *"lyre"* of his poetry.

RUMI
(Persia, 1207-1273)

THE ELUSIVE ONES

They're lovers again: Sugar dissolving in milk.
Day and night, no difference. The sun *is* the moon:
An amalgam. Their gold and silver melt together.
This is the season when the dead branch and the green
branch are the same branch.

The cynic bites his finger because he can't understand.
Omar and Ali on the same throne, two kings in one belt.
Nightmares fill with light like a holiday.
Men and angels speak one language.
The elusive ones finally meet.

The essence and the evolving forms
run to meet each other like children
to their father and mother.
Good and evil, dead and alive, everything blooms
from one natural stem.

You know this already, I'll stop.
Any direction you turn, it's one vision.
Shams, my body is a candle touched with fire.

Translated by John Moyne and Coleman Barks

Notes

The key to this poem is in the theme of the images, not in their literal meaning. Their theme is unity.

This theme has meaning from the perspective of an enlightened state of consciousness called 'unity consciousness'. In that mental state of expanded awareness, the perception of what all things have in common is so lively that it counterbalances the differences by which they are identified. That is why Rumi says: *"Any direction you turn, it's one vision."*

The simultaneous perception of an essence which is the same everywhere and yet expressed in different forms is a pleasant paradox which induces bliss and tickles one's sense of humor as one's wits stretch to accommodate the paradoxical perception. Hence Rumi's playful description.

His first two images connote the dissolution of differences and their merging, as *"sugar dissolving in milk"* and as *"lovers"* bringing two individuals into one relationship. Even opposites can be united in *"an amalgam"* and become *"the same branch"*. The rival kings, *"Omar and Ali"*, can be reconciled, and the stress of *"nightmares"* mollified with spiritual *"light"*.

All of this is possible when *"everything blooms from one natural stem."* That stem is the *"essence"* which expresses itself in *"the evolving forms"* and which makes of them *"one vision"*.

WILLIAM WORDSWORTH
(England, 1770-1850)

I SAW ONE LIFE, AND FELT THAT IT WAS JOY

Thus did my days pass on, and now at length
From Nature and her overflowing soul
I had received so much that all my thoughts
Were steeped in feeling. I was only then
Contented when with bliss ineffable
I felt the sentiment of Being spread
O'er all that moves and all that seemeth still,
O'er all that, lost beyond the reach of thought
And human knowledge, to the human eye
Invisible, yet liveth to the heart,
O'er all that leaps and runs and shouts and sings,
Or beats the gladsome air, o'er all that glides
Beneath the wave, yea, in the wave itself
And mighty depth of waters. Wonder not
If such my transports were; for in all things
I saw one life, and felt that it was joy.
One song they sang, and it was audible
Most audible then, when the fleshly ear,
O'ercome by grosser prelude of that strain,
Forgot its functions, and slept undisturbed.

Wordsworth often wrote of the effect of nature on him. He described his elevated state of mind as he wandered through the woods and fields or admired the cliffs and sky from the river down below. He drank in both the beauty and the soul of Nature, receiving in his own soul enlivenment, inspiration, happiness and a sense of the divine. Although a God-fearing man, he was not afraid to acknowledge God as feminine in Nature, as She nurtured him with *"her overflowing soul"*.

In this poem, Wordsworth describes an experience of unity. In a state of refined emotion, on the level of finest feeling, Wordsworth feels *"the sentiment of Being"*.

Wordsworth goes beyond a personal sense of Being within himself. He senses the expansiveness of *"Being"*, *"spread"* everywhere, *"O'er all"*. It is over *"all that moves and all that seemeth still"*, from the *"gladsome air"* high above to the *"depth of the waters"*. Because it is everywhere, in everything, it unifies them all.

Wordsworth describes Being from the perspective of unity consciousness. He calls it *"one life"*. He understands Being as the essence of life, the one life common to all. In his heart he knows the character of the one life, *"joy"*, the same *"bliss ineffable"* he feels within himself. The perception of Being stimulates his sense of hearing in the subtlest way, so that he transcends his usual hearing and picks up intimations of the most refined level of life, the one life, expressed in the *"One song"*.

List of Poems in Chapter Eight

Untitled
by Uvavnuk

Vacillation
by Willian Butler Yeats

God's World
by Edna St. Vincent Millay

God's Harp
by Gustav Falke

Untitled
by Shutaku

Now the Hour Bows Down
by Rainer Maria Rilke

Sweet Moment
by Hilary Huttner

Forgotten
by Octavio Paz

The Prisoner
by Emily Brontë

Heart of God
by Vachel Lindsay

In Old Age
by Judah Halevi

He Walketh by Day
Traditional Egyptian

Songs of Kabir, II. 40
by Kabir

8

MYSTICAL DELIGHTS

Mystical delights are forms of spiritual bliss. When bliss enlivens the soul, mystics feel a universal, eternal life within themselves. When bliss enlivens the thinking mind, mystics have intuitive knowledge and visions. When bliss enlivens the senses, mystics appreciate the outer world more vividly; they see and hear the divine glory or intelligence in creation, both with their eyes open and with their eyes closed in a state of subtle perception. When bliss enlivens the emotions, mystics throb with love, ecstasy and sympathy for life. When bliss enlivens speech, mystics teach wisdom. When bliss enlivens action, mystics bless, heal and are in harmony with the divine way.

Spiritual bliss comes from spirit, not just from individual spirituality but from a universal source. Though the mystic's personality and physiology color the experience, these filters are not the origin of the experience. Mystical delights arise when the mystic tunes into the bliss of creation. It is an innocent experience, as was Uvavnuk's:

The sky and the strong wind
have moved the spirit inside me
till I am carried away
trembling with joy.

The universal bliss of creation is the origin of the *"joy"* of the eternal *"one life"* that Wordsworth saw uniting all earthly life, when he wrote his poem *I Saw One Life, and Felt That It Was Joy.* It is the origin of the *"Happiness"* that Whitman found within himself in his *Song of Myself.* It is the origin of the essence Denise Levertov discovered in nature:

So absolute, it is
no other than
happiness itself, a breathing
too quiet to hear.

The mystic participates in the universal bliss. The participation may be as simple as an aesthetic sense of the beauty and order of nature, or as confusing as energy shaking the body, as awe-filled as hearing the divine vibrations that govern creation, or as ecstatic as the union between two lovers. Whether the experience is simple or sublime depends on how the awareness of the mystic expands to appreciate the divine level of life. There are more possibilities than can be contained in one volume.

The level of life we call divine could be understood in a less religious framework. It might be understood as the most fundamental or subtle level, a universal level, or a field of intelligence or consciousness. Whitman called it *"form, union, plan—it is eternal life"*.

Since the first vibration of creation—whether you understand it as light or divine thought or a 'big bang' or as universal consciousness moving within itself to know itself—a process of expansion or unfoldment has been going on. The mystic finds that expression imbued with bliss.

The tendency for bliss to expand is active in the individual mind, and when the mystic's own consciousness expands, it becomes more lively with bliss. This leads the mystic to share his bliss with other people and so to expand bliss into their lives. Yeats expressed it when he wrote:

It seemed, so great my happiness,
That I was blessed and could bless.

The expansion of bliss can push a person to his or her limits of comprehension and feeling. It can be a challenging experience, difficult to bear. When Edna St. Vincent Millay was enraptured by the divine beauty of nature, in all honesty she cried out:

Here such a passion is
As stretcheth me apart. Lord, I do fear
Thou'st made the world too beautiful this year.
My soul is all but out of me— Let fall
No burning leaf; prithee, let no bird call.

The world of nature is a logical focus for mystical perception because it seems engineered by an intelligence greater than our own. Nature can be appreciated with different kinds of delight. It may seem grand in a way that reminds a person of the divine even though nothing supernatural is seen consciously. Or, the play of light may become fascinating, even to the point that objects seem glowing with light. One may hear a humming or feel the elation of a soundless melody. One may perceive an abstract presence that makes everything seem more charming and more related. How nature is perceived does not depend on the landscape but on the purity of consciousness of the observer and the breadth, flexibility and subtleness of the observer's awareness.

When Gustav Falke looked out at the landscape on a moonlit night, nature was more than beautiful, it was holy. In his poem *God's Harp*, he wrote, *"A Sabbath radiance covers all the ways."* With his heightened perception, the bough of apple blossoms *"shines magically"*. Barely perceptible, *"a stranger music rings"* whose *"subtle tone"* is the vibration of *"God's harp"* and *"the song of His delight"*. Falke was able to perceive the vibration of the subtlest level of life, which emanates from the divine governance of *"His busy hand"*.

When Shutaku looked out his *"moon-filled"* window, he too saw more than beauty. Because his consciousness was steeped in truth, he saw that *"each molecule preaches perfect law"*.

Mystics are aware of the role their own consciousness plays in mystical perception. In a state of peak awareness, Rilke understood that not only is beauty in the eye of the observer but also that the observer's consciousness enlivens what he sees and brings out its hidden beauty. In a moment that is *"lucid"* and *"bold"*, when he feels his *"own power"*, then his perception molds what he sees and *"paints it large on a background of gold"*.

The power of consciousness to enliven the object of attention takes on a new importance when it is applied to human relations in the poem *"Sweet Moment"*. The flow of attention from woman to man is seen as an extension of the flow of divine consciousness pouring into creation as a creative act.

Thus mystical delights arise from the interplay of the spiritual consciousness of the mystic with the spiritual value of what he or she is perceiving. The object of perception may be an object in the outer world, or it may be an inner sensation or vision.

For the mystic, everything has a spiritual value. It is locatable at the most fundamental level of being. There the mystic finds qualities that hint of transcendence, infinity, eternity, sheer being and unity. There also the mystic finds that the divine is operative. There the mystic is awash in awe, energy and most sweetly *"a tone of love"*.

The spiritual value of human physicality is explored in the poem *Forgotten* by Octavio Paz. As the poet loses himself in the sensory experience of the body, he transcends to the level of *"infinity/ in your infinite being"* and transforms erotic ecstasy into mystical bliss.

Mystical delights can also take the form of visions. Visions may be interpreted within the context of a traditional religion, or they may be beyond cultural conventions, surprising even to the mystic.

In a visionary experience, a thought formed by an Intelligence greater than your own appears in your mind, and your mind perceives that greater thought. That thought gives you knowledge. The thought may consist of words, spoken or unspoken. Or, it may be a higher emotion, such as divine love. Or, the thought may be something to be processed by one or more of the five senses, such as a picture in your mind's eye. If the vision comes as an image, it will be brighter and sharper than your ordinary mental pictures. Unlike your own mental pictures which change as your thoughts change, the visionary image will remain constant as you observe it and think various thoughts of your own. It will only change to show you something new. It will vanish of its own accord. No memory of it is as vivid as the original experience.

Visions were a source of ecstacy for the lonely Emily Brontë. In the dead of night, her mind made more keen by fasting, she transcended her ordinary life. Her visions revealed to her the infinite and the ultimate truth. When her *"messenger of Hope"* arrived, she was pushed to her limits. She wrote, *"Winds take a pensive tone, and stars a tender fire, / And visions rise, and change, that kill me with desire"* then in *"a soundless calm"* with *"unuttered harmony, / . . . the Unseen its truth reveals"*.

The fiery American poet Vachel Lindsay was prone to religious visions. If the parade of Old Testament prophets in his youth was not enough, then *"God, the creeping fire"* who *"scorched the walls of my arteries"* must have been. In his poem *Heart of God*, Lindsay throbbed with a divine throb and found a *"wild thundering"* faith.

The medieval poet Judah Halevi also had revelations, in which spiritual sensations and intuitive knowledge were melded into the same experience. In his poem *"In Old Age"*, he states the source of his knowledge plainly:

My intellect beholds visions from the Almighty,
And I understand that the Lord is within me;
That His Precious Self is hidden,
But His works reveal Him to the eye of thought.
He kindled a lamp lit with His glory in my body;
It shows me the ways of the ancient sages.
And this is the light that grew brighter in youth,
And shines even more now that I am old.

Mystics experience God directly. The experience *"that the Lord is within me"* flowers in various forms. Almighty power, a thundering sound, energy or light in the body, a spiritual presence in the body, unearthly peace, healing love, and divine direction have been reported.

A sweet experience of God was recorded in verse by the Indian poet Kabir. Kabir advocated the path of union with God through love of God, and in his poetry he described how it worked for him. He allows himself to be *"lost in the sky of love"*, so that *"love envelopes the body and mind."* Then his beloved Lord actually is *"in this vessel of my body."*

Mystical delights are glimpses of an eternal reality whose essence is intelligence and bliss. Drawing our attention towards that reality, they inspire us to participate with full awareness.

UVAVNUK
(Eskimo, mid-19th to early 20th century)

UNTITLED

The great sea has set me in motion,
set me adrift,
moving me like a weed in a river.

The sky and the strong wind
have moved the spirit inside me
till I am carried away
trembling with joy.

Translated and adapted by Stephen Mitchell

Notes

The great sea of life has a motion, a way. What an art of life—to be moved by that current rather than swimming against it, to be part of nature, moved effortlessly with the flow of things, as naturally as *"a weed in a river"*. This is the harmony of outer behavior when one is moved by the great intelligence of Nature.

The intelligence of Nature, sensed in *"the sky"* and *"the strong wind"*, also touches the sensitive heart within and moves the inner spirit. When the spirit stirs, it experiences its own nature, which is bliss. Immediately there is an experience of joy so ecstatic that Uvavnuk feels *"carried away/ trembling with joy"*.

The translator tells us that Uvavnuk became a shaman and a healer when an electrifying experience of joy and purification befell her. A ball of fire fell from the night sky and struck her. She felt her organs and everything inside her set aglow. Had she been struck by ball lightning or by something beyond our knowledge? She ran home and began to sing a song of great joy. The other people in her house were caught up in the ecstasy. *"They lifted up their arms and let go of all darkness, all suspicion and malice. The song allowed them to blow these forces away as if they were blowing a speck of dust from the palm of ᵍir hand. Ever since then, whenever she sings this song, eⁿⁱᵃble to heal others. "*[1]

Her bᵒ ᵛnuk's experience bears some resemblance to the can bless ⁿ spiritual, kundalini energy described in yoga. enabling them ᵛ with energy. She is filled with joy. She ⁿᵛ enlivening the same power in them, ᵍₒ of their darkness. (One of the

---

1. Stephen Mitchell credits this—
Iglulik Eskimos by Knud Rasmussenᵈote to *Intellectual Culture of the* ⁿᵖenhagen, 1929.

186

effects of kundalini is to clear the mind of negative emotions and anti-social desires, just as the people surrounding Uvavnuk lifted up their arms and let go of their darkness and malice.) Uvavnuk is inspired with word and song that have the power to purify and heal. The stirring of kundalini stimulates the faculties of inspiration, language, arts, wisdom, intuition, healing and supernormal talents.

WILLIAM BUTLER YEATS
(Ireland, 1865-1939)

VACILLATION (IV)

My fiftieth year had come and gone,
I sat, a solitary man,
In a crowded London shop,
An open book and empty cup
On the marble table-top.

While on the shop and street I gazed
My body of a sudden blazed;
And twenty minutes more or less
It seemed, so great my happiness,
That I was blessed and could bless.

Notes

"The mystical life," wrote Yeats, *"is the centre of all that I do and all that I think and all that I write."*[2] Yeats was attracted to the mystical, the occult and the mythical. He admired the lectures of the Hindu Mohini Chatterji and for a few years was a member of the Theosophical Society, but it was the Hermetic Order of the Golden Dawn and its philosophy which kept his interest for thirty-five years. The Golden Dawn was a society founded by people with backgrounds in Rosicrucianism and Theosophy. Their purpose was to study occult science and wisdom, from adepts and alchemists going back through Christian Rosenkreuz to writings as old as 100-300 A.D. attributed to Hermes Trismegistos, a sage or deity who represented a blend of Egyptian and Greek mysticism and who was a patron of the written arts. The society used the term 'magic' to cover a range of activities, including a system of esoteric knowledge with a hierarchy of initiations, experiments in psychic powers, contact with guides, meditations, and rituals. Among its purposes was to *"reach up to the Divine and become one with the All self, the great One-All."*[3] In a society document, Yeats argued, *"The central principle of all the Magic of power is that everything we formulate in the imagination, if we formulate it strongly enough, realises itself in the circumstances of life, acting either through our own souls or through the spirits of nature."*[4]

When Yeats was about 52, his new bride added another influence when she began automatic writing and

2. Allan Wade, *The Letters of W. B. Yeats* (New York: Macmillan, 1955), p. 211.
3. George Mills Harper, *Yeats's Golden Dawn* (Wellingborough, Northamptonshire: Aquarian Press, 1987), p. 87.
4. *Ibid.*, p. 265.

speaking. Over the course of seven years, communications for Yeats were given through her by spirit guides who said, *"We have come to give you metaphors for poetry."*[5] Such metaphors were important to Yeats because he believed that symbols used in poetry and ritual could evoke a level of memory that was part of the one great memory of Nature herself.

Yeats' Hermetic colleagues would have understood the meaning of the *"open book"* and *"empty cup"* in his poem *"Vacillation"*. In their rituals, they used a cup to represent the element of nature. Some contemporary Rosicrucians associate the *"empty cup"* with that part of the individual which is to be filled with spiritual energy and enlightenment. The cup also resembles the alchemic vessel in which transmutation took place and also the Arthurian grail which was full of spiritual energy. In the Tarot deck, which Yeats consulted, cups represent emotion, an interpretation which anticipates the next stanza's description of the bliss associated with enlightenment. As for the book, it is associated with knowledge and wisdom.

However, because the poet was not looking at these objects but *"upon the shop and street"* when he was surprised *"of a sudden"* by a special experience of bliss, we think that the book, cup, table, shop and street were not symbols but rather the actual scene at the time that this experience happened to Yeats. Because Yeats was an elitist who looked down on the shop-keeping class and the bustle of city life, it is ironic that this blessed experience occurred in a *"crowded London shop"*. Such cosmic humor is typical of spontaneous mystical experience, and there may have been a lesson in it for Yeats.

Yeats had had similar experiences before. He wrote in *Per Amica Silentia Lunae:*

---

5. W. B. Yeats, *A Vision* (New York: Collier Books, 1965), p. 8.

At certain moments, always unforeseen, I become happy, most commonly when at hazard I have opened some book of verse. . . . I look at the strangers near as if I had known them all my life . . . : everything fills me with affection . . . It may be an hour before the mood passes, but latterly I seem to understand that I enter upon it the moment I cease to hate.[6]

In *Vacillation,* Yeats' joy and blessedness and his sensation that *"My body of a sudden blazed"* indicate a classic experience of spiritual energy. The yogis have a name for this energy when it stirs in the body—kundalini. When it stirs along the spine, tingling, heat or light may be sensed in an esoteric center of the body or throughout the whole, as the energy enlivens every nerve, every cell, every organ. One may feel physically stronger. The rarefied physiology supports a rarefied consciousness and a variety of mystical delights. A typical experience is bliss—a combination of *"happiness"* and that sheen of spirituality which Yeats calls *"blessed"*.

Yeats' report that *"It seemed, so great my happiness,/ That I was blessed and could bless"* is a clue to a greater mystery, the phenomenon of cosmic bliss. This bliss is larger than the individual; it does not depend on events in the individual's life. In moments of clarity, the individual samples it. It is like a background field of universal consciousness which is experienced at times by individual consciousness.

The blissful person becomes a point of further expansion of the bliss into other people. This is why Yeats writes both that *"I was blessed and could bless."* The urge to extend blessing and bliss feels as though it comes from the cosmic bliss itself, to make life like itself.

---

6. Virginia Moore, *The Unicorn* (New York: Macmillan Company, 1954), p. 404. Quoting *Essays* by W. B. Yeats, p. 533.

EDNA ST. VINCENT MILLAY
(United States, 1892-1950)

GOD'S WORLD

O world, I cannot hold thee close enough!
  Thy winds, thy wide gray skies!
  Thy mists, that roll and rise!
Thy woods, this autumn day, that ache and sag
And all but cry with color! That gaunt crag
To crush! To lift the lean of that black bluff!
World, world! I cannot get thee close enough!

Long have I known a glory in it all
  But never knew I this,
  Here such a passion is
As stretcheth me apart. Lord, I do fear
Thou'st made the world too beautiful this year.
My soul is all but out of me— Let fall
No burning leaf; prithee, let no bird call.

Notes

A master poet, Edna St. Vincent Millay puts into words the appreciation of Nature which many people feel but can hardly find the words to equal it. Amidst the beauty of nature, there is a sense of seeing God's handiwork, and so the woods are described not as a random collection of sticks but as *"Thy"* woods, the woods of God.

Seeing the world as God's handiwork is a stretch. *"Here such a passion is/ As stretcheth me apart."* There is some aching feeling to stretching to such a high perception and intense emotion; even the trees seem to *"ache"* and *"cry with color"*. In her ecstatic perception, the world is *"too beautiful"* because her aesthetic sense is being stretched to appreciate the sublime dimension. Everything has such *"a glory"* that the poet wants more, crying *"World, world! I cannot get thee close enough!"* Yet she can hardly bear the delight of it.

GUSTAV FALKE
(Germany, 1853-1916)

GOD'S HARP

The wind, stirring in the dark foliage, brings
Songs to me of the wakeful nightingale;
At intervals, a stranger music rings.
Whence are these voices that now light,
Now deeply echo from the night
And now of their own beauty fail?

The apple bough of white,
That at my open window rocks and sways,
Against the pane its dewy blossom lays,
Shines magically in the blanched light.
A Sabbath radiance covers all the ways.
My vision waxes vast and wide:

Oh, there arises now a solemn tide
For those who live in dreams, the delicate
Souls that to every subtle tone vibrate,
Which from God's harp rings forth
And prophesies that he forever
His busy hand in ancient music plies,
And will not end the song of His delight.

Thus ends it never—
Hark, what a tone of love passed through the night!

Translated by Ludwig Lewisohn

In the stillness of the night, the poet hears the *"music"* of *"God's harp"*. His sense of hearing is responding to the Infinite, giving him the impression of hearing subtle tones that fade in and out of perception. He concludes that these are heard by *"delicate souls"* who *"vibrate"* with that same, *"solemn tide"* of eternal life from which the *"ancient music"* springs.

The sound of *"God's harp"* is the sound of the divine vibrations which create and maintain the manifest world. These vibrations have been described in various ways by various people, sometimes as bells, flutes, violins or harps, as full chords or the long tones of the music of the spheres, sometimes as heavenly hymns or the song of creation, sometimes as rumbling, thunder, rushing water, the hum of bees or the cosmic motor of Om, sometimes as the whisperings of intelligences or the hubbub of the laws of nature functioning, sometimes as divine words which are simultaneously sound and light. As Western physics has proposed that all is particle-wave energy, so Indian metaphysics has proposed that all is ultimately vibration and that the vibration has a subtle sound-value which can be perceived.

The poet is sensitive to this level of life when he is in a state of heightened appreciation, enjoying the magic of the *"Sabbath radiance"*. This radiance is more than the moonlight to which it is naturally compared. It has the holy quality of the Sabbath, a day of spiritual retreat, and the silvery luster of the inner light that illumines the visual perception of mystics.

One can appreciate the divine through any sense. The stimulation of the sense of hearing brings to the poet's mind metaphors of music, song and tone that express something more abstract at their basis. The poet understands their true nature. It is divine *"delight"* and *"love"*. How wonderful that the poet was awake to hear *"what a tone of love passed through the night!"*

SHUTAKU
(Japan, Fourteenth Century)

UNTITLED

Mind set free in the Dharma-realm,
I sit at the moon-filled window
Watching the mountains with my ears,
Hearing the stream with open eyes.
Each molecule preaches perfect law,
Each moment chants true sutra:
The most fleeting thought is timeless,
A single hair's enough to stir the sea.

Translated by Lucien Stryk and Takashi Ikemoto

Notes

This Buddhist poem describes a quintessential experience of abstract meditation. The poet's mind attains a universal state, the *"Dharma-realm"* of absolute, pure consciousness. His mind feels *"free"*, unbounded as universal consciousness and free from ignorance.

The poet reports *"watching the mountains"* with his *"ears"* and *"hearing the stream"* with his *"eyes"*. A mixture of the senses like this is called synesthesia. It crops up occasionally in religious experiences, as in Cardinal Newman's untitled poem which is discussed in the chapter *Awakening*. Ordinarily, when the senses are applied to finite things, they stay within their finite boundaries. But when the senses are applied to the Infinite, the rules change. Why? 1) Because in entering a meditative state of consciousness, the mystic is using his mind and physiology in a new way and 2) because the stimulation that flows through the channels of the senses is so unusual that it produces results which have a metaphorical quality. In Shutaku's case, with his mind *"set free"*, he has turned his attention to the subtle stimulation of the transcendental value of the *"Dharma-realm"*. What he sees with his ears and hears with his eyes has no sight and no sound: it is abstract *"perfect law"* that he senses in each *"molecule"*! What he is sensing is real; it is infinite Intelligence in action. When his attention turns to the *"mountains"* and the *"stream"*, his senses act in an interchangeable way that indicates he is grappling with the Infinite.

Seeing the infinite in the finite, his mind takes on the qualities of the Infinite. As the Infinite is eternal, his thought becomes *"timeless"*. As the almighty Infinite interrelates everything, he feels that even something as small as a single hair or a single thought is *"enough to stir the sea"* of universal consciousness.

RAINER MARIA RILKE
(Europe, in German, 1875-1926)

NOW THE HOUR BOWS DOWN

Now the hour bows down, it touches me, throbs
metallic, lucid and bold:
my senses are trembling. I feel my own power—
on the plastic day I lay hold.

Until I perceived it, no thing was complete,
but waited, hushed, unfulfilled.
My vision is ripe, to each glance like a bride
comes softly the thing that was willed.

There is nothing too small, but my tenderness paints
it large on a background of gold,
and I prize it, not knowing whose soul at the sight,
released, may unfold. . .

Translated by Babette Deutsch

Notes

    This is the opening poem in Rilke's *The Book of Hours*, which is a collection of religious speculations.
    In this poem, the poet describes a state of heightened alertness. Keenly he feels the present moment, which

seems *"lucid and bold"*. His physical senses *"are trembling"* with excitement. There is a sense of efficacy, *"my own power"*, which can mold *"the plastic day"* as easily as Rodin, whom Rilke admired deeply, could model his sculptures.

When the lively attention of the poet falls upon an inanimate object, a mysterious thing happens: The object becomes enlivened. The medium of enlivenment is what the observer and the object have in common, a field of universal consciousness. Even the inanimate object in its *"hushed, unfulfilled"* state has at its basis an essence of energy and universal intelligence. The observer also has at his basis an essence of universal intelligence which is more expressed in him because of his state of heightened alertness. When the lively observer and the observed object come together in a moment when his *"vision is ripe"*, the universal essence that they have in common becomes a lively part of the experience. This is one explanation of how the attention of the observer enlivens the object.

Another perspective comes from quantum physics, which views reality as a probability. Before a quantum event is measured, its probability is *"unfulfilled"* because it is not yet observed to be a specific event. When observed, the quantum wave is collapsed into a specific event. Generalizing from this view, one may speculate that all of reality is a probability that collapses into a specific reality when observed by a specific consciousness and that the reality you get may vary according to your state of consciousness.

In any case, how fully the object is appreciated depends upon the observer. Rilke's *"tender"* way of seeing glorifies the object, as though it were painted *"large on a background of gold"*. The *"gold"* may be a hint of the golden glow that is sometimes seen by mystics.

HILARY HUTTNER
(United States, 1951-)

SWEET MOMENT

The miracle of today, it is warm in November.
The moon rises white in the late afternoon.
The clouds really are pink as cotton candy.
The sky really is blue as a lagoon.

The outdoor air and the indoor air
Blend together in the quiet café.
Two people are talking by the window.
No, he is talking; she is listening,
Listening so intently, she is still as a picture.

She is making him great by listening.
She is far too busy to hear.
She is pouring out her attention,
As the goddess pours love into her creation,
To make a child, to make a goddess,
To make a circle that lasts forever.

The sunset slants through the window.
The lamps are lit to welcome the evening.
But one cannot say whether the light
Is shining on her face or her face is shining.

Notes

In this *"sweet moment"* on a Californian afternoon, male and female meet, and love inspires the flow of pure consciousness into active life.

The sky displays signs of what is to come: the *"pink"* color of the female, the *"blue"* color of the male, and the *"white"* color that unites all colors. The moon symbolizes pure consciousness and female, yin energy, while the sun symbolizes male, yang energy. The male, exterior *"air"* and the female, interior air *"blend together"* in the café.

The couple sitting by the window are engaged in a conversational dance which is not about words but about attention. As the young woman listens, her special quietude gives her access to pure consciousness. Her attention focuses that consciousness on the man, enlivening his own consciousness, *"making him great"*.

This process is likened to a microcosm of the macrocosmic process of the creative flow of divine consciousness. Poetically, the divine is called *"goddess"*. Technically, it might be called the expressive, creative, sustaining, blessing aspect of the Godhead. The flow of divine consciousness creates the macrocosm. The flow of consciousness from woman to man is also creative; it will create a relationship that leads to the union of the sexes and procreation. This will complete the *"circle"* which lasts *"forever"* because it continues on through the generations.

The woman's face *"is shining"* with the glow of the consciousness that she has been radiating to the man. This shining which comes at a time of energy and bliss may be the visible product of a spiritual energy. It may also be facilitated by ojas, a most refined substance produced in the body which mediates bliss. At peak moments, the faces of mystics are known to shine.

FORGOTTEN

Close your eyes and lose yourself in shadows
under the shadows of your eyelids' red-leaf forest.

Go down among those spirals
of sound humming and falling
and sounding faraway, remote,
all the way to the eardrum,
a deafened waterfall.

Send your self down to the shadows,
drown yourself in your skin,
further, in your entrails:
let the bone, with its livid spark,
dazzle and blind you,
and among chasms and the gulfs of shadow
open its blue panache, will-o-wisp.

And in this liquid shadow of the dream
now bathe your nakedness;
relinquish your form, your foam
(nobody knows who flung it on the shore);
lose yourself in your self, infinity
in your infinite being,
sea losing itself in another sea:
forget yourself and forget me.

In that forgetfulness ageless and endless
lips, kisses, love, all, born again:
the stars are daughters of the night.

Translated by Muriel Rukeyser

Notes

Because there is a similarity between sexual and spiritual ecstasy, a description of one can be taken for a description of the other. For Octavio Paz, however, sexual ecstasy was spiritual ecstasy. Paz wrote that love was an *"authentic erotic communion"* in which the lover aspired *"to realize oneself in the other"* in *"a perpetual discovery, an immersion in the waters of reality and a constant recreation".*[7] Literary critic Jason Wilson wrote of Paz and his views on orgasm that Paz *"pinned man's identity to that ecstatic experience whose intensity is a glimpse of paradise. . . . an inner experience of liberation."*[3]

In this poem, Paz begins a journey of transcendence by exploring subtler levels of awareness of the physical body. *"Go down"*, he says, spiraling into an inner state, like a mystic traveler following the hum of an inner sound. Let your senses be dazzled by the vividness of it. Then *"lose"* the boundaries of yourself to find *"your infinite being"*. And in that transcendence, *"that forgetfulness, ageless and endless"*, find *"all, born again"*.

Paz *"read deeply in Zen, Buddhism, Tantra, Chinese painting"*[8] and Japanese poetry. In Tantra, Paz must have found a philosophy of interest. Among other things, Tantra views the world as the result of the interplay and union of opposites. One of its techniques uses the union of the opposite sexes. Seeing each other as the expression of the divine male Shiva and the divine female Shakti, uniting in one divine reality, a man and a woman lie together nude for half an hour, genitals touching, to create a bio-energy to further spiritual advancement.[9]

---

7. Jason Wilson, *Octavio Paz* (Boston: G. K. Hall, 1986), pp. 55-56.
8. *Ibid.*, p. 70.
9. Omar Garrison, *Tantra: The Yoga of Sex* (New York: Julian Press, 1983), pp. 112-116 passim.

EMILY BRONTE
(England, 1818-1848)

THE PRISONER

Still, let my tyrants know, I am not doomed to wear
Year after year in gloom, and desolate despair;
A messenger of Hope comes every night to me,
And offers for short life, eternal liberty.

He comes with western winds, with evening's wandering
        airs,
With that clear dusk of heaven that brings the thickest
        stars.
Winds take a pensive tone, and stars a tender fire,
And visions rise, and change, that kill me with desire.

Desire for nothing known in my maturer years,
When Joy grew mad with awe, at counting future tears.
When, if my spirit's sky was full of flashes warm,
I knew not whence they came, from sun or thunder-storm.

But, first, a hush of peace—a soundless calm descends;
The struggle of distress, and fierce impatience ends;
Mute music soothes my breast—unuttered harmony,
That I could never dream, till Earth was lost to me.

Then dawns the Invisible; the Unseen its truth reveals;
My outward sense is gone, my inward essence feels:
Its wings are almost free—its home, its harbour found,
Measuring the gulf, it stoops and dares the final bound.

O! dreadful is the check—intense the agony—
When ear begins to hear, and the eye begins to see;

When the pulse begins to throb, the brain to think again;
The soul to feel the flesh, and the flesh to feel the chain.

Yet I would lose no sting, would wish no torture less;
The more that anguish racks, the earlier it will bless;
And robed in fires of hell, or bright with heavenly shine,
If it but herald death, the vision is divine!

Notes

Emily Brontë was a creator of satisfying fictions for her private daydreams, her poems and her novel *Wuthering Heights*. Her inner realms held such charm that her imaginings were her real life. Ordinary intercourse with the external world was too painful for her.

To the external world, her life seemed limited and lonely. She spent most of her thirty years in her father's remote parsonage on the edge of a Yorkshire moor, writing in the privacy of night. A modern biographer tells us:

"The darkness of night, like fasting, made Emily feel she transcended the demands and even all awareness of her body. She became a 'space-sweeping' or 'chainless soul' governed by a 'God of Visions' who delivered her from the 'shattered prison' of her body."[10]

In her poem *The Prisoner*, Emily Brontë defies the imprisoning dreariness of her staid life. She reveals a secret bliss that is a spiritual *"liberty"*. Who or what is the herald of this spiritual experience, the *"messenger of Hope"* who comes at night to this lonely woman? Then the tone of the experience becomes *"pensive"* and *"tender"* and visionary. *"Visions rise, and change, that kill me with desire."*

She enters a spiritual state, with classic physiological and psychological symptoms. First comes *"peace"* and *"calm"* in body and mind, as the *"struggle of distress . . . ends"*. In that inner peace, she experiences a *"harmony"* that is too subtle for words and sound but which has the

---

10. Katherine Frank, *A Chainless Soul* (Boston: Houghton Mifflin, 1990), p. 105.

soothing, aesthetic quality of music, as though she were perceiving a divine harmony.

Then she senses the Divine behind the harmony, *"the Invisible; the Unseen its truth reveals"*. This perception is possible because her senses have turned from the *"outward"* material world to the *"inward"* realm of the spirit or *"essence"*. She recognizes the *"truth"* of the *"Unseen"* and the *"home"* of her *"inward essence"*. Drawn towards that home, she attempts to dare the *"final bound"*.

Alas, she is brought back into mundane reality by the limitations of her body.[11] Her body had been in a state of deep *"peace"*, the suspension that is conducive to mystic experience. Then her physiology reasserts itself:

O! dreadful is the check—intense the agony—
When ear begins to hear, and the eye begins to see;
When the pulse begins to throb, the brain to think
*   again;*
The soul to feel the flesh, and the flesh to feel the
*   chain.*

Emily Brontë suffered from the contrast between the bliss of her mystic vision and the mundane, physical reality which she scorned. She was unable to integrate the two. We realize how important that integration is when we compare her unhappy life with the fulfillment described by other poets.

---

11. Physical limitation, leading to a return to non-mystical, physical activity, is the usual cause that brings a mystic back out of transcendence. That is why mystics of India and Asia seek to culture the body and its subtle structures, making the nervous system, breathing and metabolism more flexible.

VACHEL LINDSAY
(United States, 1879-1932)

HEART OF GOD

O great heart of God,
Once vague and lost to me,
Why do I throb with your throb tonight,
In this land, eternity?

O little heart of God,
Sweet intruding stranger,
You are laughing in my human breast,
A Christ-child in a manger.

Heart, dear heart of God,
Beside you now I kneel,
Strong heart of faith. O heart not mine,
Where God has set His seal.

Wild thundering heart of God,
Out of my doubt I come,
And my foolish feet with prophets' feet,
March with the prophets' drum.

Notes

Vachel Lindsay was a self-styled religious thinker, blending a strong Protestant background with his own cosmology of redemption (illustrated with A Map of the Universe) and an admiration for the Buddha. In his *War Bulletin Number Three*, he spelled out his beliefs in his essay *"The Creed of a Beggar"*. He wrote:

> *I believe in God, the creeping fire. I have met him. He has scorched the walls of my arteries. . . I believe in Christ the Socialist, for I have seen the Sermon on the Mount many times illustrated by my hosts on the road. . . I believe in that perilous maddening flower, the Holy Ghost, the most dangerous bloom in the Universe, I have eaten of it.*

Lindsay was prone to religious visions. They began in boyhood, when *"one night Lindsay saw the prophets in a corner of his room pass by clothed in gorgeous apparel. Another time he saw them in the same garb in front of an elm tree."*[12] Later, he wrote in his *Preface* to *The Tramp's Excuse and other Poems:*

> *In September 1906, on the boat returning from Europe, about two o'clock in the morning, I was awakened by the overwhelming vision of Christ as a Shepherd, singing on a hill. The first three stanzas of the poem I Heard Immanuel Singing were half formed in my mind before I woke, and I said aloud, "I have found my God." I felt at the time that this experience had more right to authority over me than any previous picture in the air. It came with terrible power.*

---

12. Edgar Lee Masters, *Vachel Lindsay* (New York: Charles Scribner's Sons, 1935), p. 213 and p. 208.

JUDAH HALEVI
(Spain, in Hebrew, 1075-1141)

IN OLD AGE

I rouse my slumbering thoughts
To lull the cravings of my heart and eyes.
I delve into the past
To tell my ears what the future will be.
Then my mind's lips tell me of great things
And set the marvel of my Rock before me.
They disclose to me deep mysteries,
Until I believe that I dwell among the angels.

My intellect beholds visions from the Almighty,
And I understand that the Lord is within me;
That His Precious Self is hidden,
But His works reveal Him to the eye of thought.
He kindled a lamp lit with His glory in my body;
It shows me the ways of the ancient sages.
And this is the light that grew brighter in youth,
And shines even more now that I am old.

Translated by P. T. Carmi

Judah Halevi (or ha-Levi, the Levite) lived in Spain at a time when the Jewish community there enjoyed a Golden Age. This poem, which tells of revelations that *"disclose to me deep mysteries"* and *"visions from the Almighty"* is consistent with Halevi's premise that the religion of Judaism rests firstly on revelation. Perhaps his premise and his appreciation for Biblical revelation grew out of his experience of personal revelation.

Halevi describes a prophetic state that tells of *"the future"* and *"great things"*. The basis of this state is closeness to God, *"the marvel of my Rock before me"*. He feels that he is on a heavenly plane, *"that I dwell among the angels"*.

In this state, he *"beholds visions"* that he describes as bursts of intuitive knowledge rather than as visual tableaus. The knowledge that comes to him is mystical. It is a sense of the Creator in the creation. He also feels a divine energy in his body, *"a lamp lit with His glory in my body"*. The oil-burning lamp evokes associations of the warmth of spiritual energy, the flame of the heart center, the light of the mind, and the lamp of eternal light in the Jewish temple. The divine energy enlightens his consciousness, showing him *"the ways of the ancient sages"*. It is one of the secrets of his genius.

TRADITIONAL EGYPTIAN SCRIPTURE
(Egypt, circa 4266-3300 B.C.)

HE WALKETH BY DAY

I am Yesterday, Today and Tomorrow,
The Divine Hidden Soul who created the gods
And who feedeth the blessed.

I am Lord of the Risers from Death,
Whose Forms are the lamps in the House of the Dead,
Whose shrine is the Earth.

When the sky is illumined with crystal,
Then gladden my road and broaden my path
And clothe me in light.

Keep me safe from the Sleeper in Darkness,
When eventide closeth the eyes of the god
And the door by the wall.

In the dawn I have opened the Sycamore;
My Form is the form of all women and men,
My spirit is God.

Translated by Robert Hillyer

Notes

The last line of this hymn holds the key to its meaning: *"My spirit is God."*

This hymn is from the ancient papyrus *Chapters of Coming Forth by Day.* Because a copy of this book was buried in tombs with the dead, its modern discoverers have dubbed it *The Egyptian Book of the Dead.*

Chapters of Coming Forth by Day is a manual to guide the soul to immortality. The technique of the manual is a series of affirmations, often with the format *"I am . . .".* The dead person's soul arises and uses the affirmations to journey through spiritual realms, to transform itself, to identify itself with the divine, and to gain knowledge and immortality.

In the spiritual journey, the dead person is judged in the Hall of Judgment. If he is successful in affirming that he is free from sin and worldly attachments, his heart will be lightweight on the scales of justice, and he will be judged True of Word and of Quiet Heart. Through affirmations, he takes on spiritual qualities and becomes one with the Egyptian deities, as in the hymn *He Maketh Himself One with The Only God Whose Limbs Are the Many Gods.* He becomes pure as the lotus. Thus he affirms his mastery, avoids obstacles, passes in peace, and establishes his soul in the realm of everlastingness.

How old this hymn is we do not know. At least one of the *Chapters* is dated to a remodeling project in 4266 B.C., when a construction foreman discovered the chapter in the foundation of a statue.[13] Other chapters may have been composed earlier in an oral tradition or as much as a thousand years later.

---

13. Brian Brown, *The Wisdom of the Egyptians* (New York: Brentano's, 1923), p. 127.

The religious experience of the Egyptian hymns may seem strange to modern readers. We are used to worshipping God as separate from ourselves. In *Chapters of Coming Forth by Day*, there is a dual approach to the divine: On the one hand, the gods are worshipped with homage as separate from oneself, as in these opening lines from the first hymn of the *Chapters*:

Homage to thee, O Ra, at thy tremendous rising!
Thou risest! Thou shinest! The Heavens are
*   rolled aside!*
Thou art the King of Gods, thou art
*   the All-comprising,*
From thee we come, in thee are deified.
Thy priests go forth at dawn;
They wash their hearts with laughter.

On the other hand, the spirit of the worshipper can progress from homage to the experience of identification with the deity. This identification is not usurping the role of the god but taking on its qualities, as a son identifies with his father and takes on his qualities and calls himself by the last name of his father. The translator expresses this well in the line *"From thee we come, in thee are deified."*

In the preceding hymns, the soul of the dead person has been resurrected and has become *"The Child of Light who findeth his Father in the Evening"*. In *He Walketh by Day*, the soul affirms that he has made himself one with the sun-god Ra, the lord of *"Yesterday, Today and Tomorrow"*, and with Osiris, *"Lord of the Risers from Death"*. The soul's declarations sound so much like the god in which he is deified that readers would not know who was speaking if they were not aware of the preceding hymns. The soul affirms about his own nature what is true of the deity:

I am Yesterday, Today and Tomorrow,

The Divine Hidden Soul who created the gods
And who feedeth the blessed.

Because the spiritual journey is not yet complete, the risen spirit of the dead person is still subject to downfall and prays to be clothed in light and kept safe from darkness and the sleep of death, during the night when the stars come out (*"when the sky is illumined with crystal"*).

In the light of dawn, he is proud of his mastery. He has mastered (*"opened"*) the key meaning of the two turquoise sycamore trees that accompany Ra as the sun-god rises. He has also discovered his universal nature, declaring:

My Form is the form of all women and men,
My spirit is God.

Was the spiritual journey of the *Chapters of Coming Forth by Day* just a hopeful myth, or was it connected to a living, religious experience? It is a likely guess that some ancient seekers were too curious about spiritual realms to wait for death to reveal the secrets of the soul.

KABIR
(India, 1440-1518)

SONGS OF KABIR, II. 40

The shadows of evening fall thick
      and deep, and the darkness of
      love envelopes the body and mind.
Open the window to the west, and be
      lost in the sky of love;
Drink the sweet honey that steeps the
      petals of the lotus of the heart.
Receive the waves in your body: what
      splendour is in the region of the sea!
Hark! The sounds of conches and
      bells are rising.
Kabir says: "O brother, behold! the
      Lord is in this vessel of my
      body."

Translated by Rabindranath Tagore

Notes

Here is a beautiful and sensuous poem typical of India. Kabir was an amalgam of the religious traditions of India, having been raised a Moslem and influenced by a Hindu guru. Out of this background, he synthesized his own path, which he popularized as 'simple yoga'.

Kabir's poem is about bhakti, the love for God which uplifts the devotee to a state of even greater appreciation of God. The *"darkness of love"* is the abstract, eyes-closed, mystical state that excludes the ordinary affairs of the day. The *"sky"* of love is the unboundedness of that state. The *"window to the west"* is the opening to that other-worldly state of mind.

The *"sweet honey"*, although it may be just a reference to the sweet bliss of the experience, is probably a more esoteric reference to a yogic nectar, a subtle substance that may be visualized as golden or tasted as sweetness during meditation when one has a celestial perception of the subtlest level of relative life. The nectar is traditionally said to be the most refined substance which mediates between the immaterial and the material and enables bliss to be expressed in the body. Kabir experiences it in the *"heart"* chakra, a spiritual center located about chest-level in the body. In the heart chakra, he finds another subtle structure, a many-petaled configuration called a *"lotus"*. (The ordinary lotus flower has concentric rings of petals.)

The *"waves"* are waves of energy. The rising sound of bells is probably more that the coursing of blood through the ear. It may be an example of celestial hearing, an experience similar to the heavenly bells that some people hear when they fall in love, for Kabir is in a state of divine love. Or, the bells and conches may be heralds of an important event: the presence of the Lord in the body of the devotee.

The experience of receiving the Lord in the vessel of the body is common to many mystics. For Kabir, it is a blissful experience. It is also like a feeling of warm water, both within the body (as water in a *"vessel"*) and surrounding the body (as in *"the regions of the sea"*), so that it feels sometimes as though the spirit of the Lord is in the body and sometimes as though the body is in the spirit of the Lord.

CONCLUSION

This concludes our tour of mystical experiences. Many more mystical poems await discovery. We hope this book will inspire further explorations of how the works of the poets reflect higher states of consciousness.

The poets challenge us to read by the light of the consciousness with which they wrote. When we appreciate the quickened spirit which inspired the poets, we will understand the grasp great poetry has on our souls.

ACKNOWLEDGMENTS

If there is any wisdom in this book, it must have begun with the author's training as a teacher of the Transcendental Meditation Program. From the lectures of Maharishi Mahesh Yogi, the author learned a modern version of ancient Vedic science, including an understanding of absolute existence, developmental stages of higher consciousness and the analysis of meditative experiences. Years later, this made it easier for the author to analyze the mystical experiences of the poets, even though the literary analysis was based on the content of the poets' writings.

In over twelve years of research for this book, the librarians of Palo Alto, California and Nevada were invaluable in their help in digging up background material about the poets. They were all patient, competent and always willing to do as much work as was needed.

I would especially like to thank my husband Daniel who read rough drafts of the manuscript to add his suggestions for improvement.

Finally, thanks goes to the poets, their heirs and copyright holders for permission to reprint the wonderful poems that are the reason for this book.

COPYRIGHT SOURCES

Poems in Chapter 3

Chosen Site by Shuntaro Tanikawa, translated by Harold Wright. From the book *The Selected Poems of Shuntaro Tanikawa* translated by Harold Wright (San Francisco: North Point Press, 1983), p. 105. Copyright 1983 by Harold Wright. Reprinted by permission of Farrar, Straus & Giroux, 19 Union Square, New York, NY 10003.

The Holy Longing by Johann Wolfgang von Goethe, translated by Robert Bly. From the book *News of the Universe* by Robert Bly, p. 70. Copyright 1980 by Robert Bly. Reprinted by permission of Sierra Club Books, 100 Bush St., 13th Floor, San Francisco, CA 94104.

Stanzas Concerning an Ecstasy Experienced in High Contemplation by San Juan de la Cruz, translated by K. Kavanaugh and O. Rodrigues. From the book *The Collected Works of St. John of the Cross* translated by Kieran Kavanaugh and Otilio Rodriguez. Copyright 1979, 1991 by Washington Province of Discalced Carmelites. Reprinted by permission of I. C. S. Publications, 2131 Lincoln Rd., N.E., Washington, D.C. 20002 USA.

Tea at the Palaz of Hoon by Wallace Stevens. From the book *The Palm at the End of the Mind* by Wallace Stevens, p. 54. Copyright 1967, 1969, 1971 by Holly Stevens. Reprinted by permission of Alfred A. Knopf, Inc., a subsidiary of Random House, Inc., 201 E. 50th St., New York, NY 10022.

The Curative Powers of Silence by Al Young. From the book *The Song Turning Back Into Itself* by Al Young (New York: Holt, Rinehart & Winston, 1971), pp. 42-43. Copyright 1965, 1966, 1967, 1968, 1970, 1971 by Al

Young. Reprinted by permission of Henry Holt & Co., Inc., 115 W. 18th St., New York, NY 10011.

If only there were stillness by Rainer Maria Rilke, translated by Babette Deutsch. From the book *Rainier Maria Rilke: Poems from the Book of Hours*, translated by Babette Deutsch, p. 15. Copyright 1941 by New Directions. Reprinted by permission of New Directions Publishing Corp., 80 8th Ave., New York, NY 10011.

Shores of silence, part 1 by Karol Wojtyla, translated by Jerzy Peterkiewicz. From the book *Collected Poems: Karol Wojtyla* translated by Jerzy Peterkiewicz, p. 5. Copyright 1979, 1982 by Libreria Editrice Vaticana, Vatican City. Reprinted by permission of Random House, Inc., 201 E. 50th St., New York, NY 10022.

Lines, Composed a Few Miles above Tintern Abbey by William Wordsworth, *The Infinite* by Giacomo Leopardi, *A Song* by Richard Crashaw, *Song of the Prophet to the San Juan River* by Traditional Navaho, *Prayer* by George Herbert, and *Gitanjali (CIII)* by Rabindranath Tagore are in the public domain.

Poems in Chapter 4

Below Freezing by Tomas Tranströmer, translated by Robert Bly. From the book *Truth Barriers* by Robert Bly, p. 32. Copyright 1980 by Robert Bly. Reprinted by permission of Sierra Club Books, 100 Bush St., 13th Floor, San Francisco, CA 94104.

Alto Song by Hilary Huttner. Copyright 1995 by Frontline Systems, Inc. Reprinted by permission of Frontline Systems, Inc., P. O. Box 4288, Incline, NV 89450.

#22, Untitled by Juan Ramón Jiménez, translated by Eloise Roach. From the book *Juan Ramón Jiménez: Three Hundred Poems 1903-1953* translated by Eloise Roach, p.

25.   Copyright 1962 by University of Texas Press. Reprinted by permission of the University of Texas Press, P. O. Box 7819, Austin, TX 78713-7819.

Excerpt from Milarepa Tells His Story by Milarepa, translated by Lama Kunga Rimpoche and Brian Cutillo. From the book *Drinking the Mountain Stream* by Lama Kunga Rimpoche and Brian Cutillo (Novato: Lotsawa, 1978) p. 46.   Copyright 1978 by Lama Kunga Rimpoche and Brian Cutillo.   Reprinted by permission of Wisdom Publications, 361 Newbury St., Boston, MA 02115.

#57, Untitled by Han-shan, translated by Burton Watson.   From the book *Cold Mountain* translated by Burton Watson, p. 75.   Copyright 1970 by Columbia University Press.   Reprinted by permission of Columbia University Press, 562 W. 113 St., New York, NY 10025.

Dover Beach by Matthew Arnold, *How Sweet the Moonlight* by William Shakespeare, and *The World Is Too Much with Us* by William Wordsworth are in the public domain.

Poems in Chapter 5

When I Am Not Dead by John Ciardi.   From the book *In Fact* by John Ciardi (New Jersey: Rutgers University Press, 1962), p. 40.   Copyright 1962 by John Ciardi. Reprinted by permission of the Ciardi family.

Shadows by D. H. Lawrence.   From the book *The Complete Poems of D. H. Lawrence* edited by Angelo Ravagli and C. M. Wekley (New York: Viking Penguin, 1964), pp. 304-305.   Copyright 1964, 1971 by Angelo Ravagli and C. M. Weekley, Executors of the Estate of Frieda Lawrence Ravagli.   Reprinted by permission of Viking Penguin, a division of Penguin Books USA Inc., 40 W. 23rd St., New York, NY 10010.

The Latest Freed Man by Wallace Stevens.   From the book *The Palm at the End of the Mind* by Wallace Stevens,

p. 165-166. Copyright 1967, 1969, 1971 by Holly Stevens. Reprinted by permission of Alfred A. Knopf, Inc., a subsidiary of Random House, Inc., 201 E. 50th St., New York, NY 10022.

Full Moon by Tu Fu, translated by Kenneth Rexroth. From the book *One Hundred Poems from the Chinese* by Kenneth Rexroth, p. 28. Copyright 1971 by Kenneth Rexroth. Reprinted by permission of New Directions Publishing Corp., 80 8th Ave., New York, NY 10011.

i thank You God for most this amazing by e. e. cummings. From the book *Complete Poems: 1904-1962 by E. E. Cummings*, edited by George J. Firmage. Copyright (c) 1950, 1978, 1991 by the Trustees for the E. E. Cummings Trusts. Copyright (c) 1979 by George James Firmage. Reprinted by permission of Liveright Publishing Corporation, 500 Fifth Ave., New York, NY 10110.

The List by Michael McClure. From the book *Antechamber and Other Poems* by Michael McClure, p. 165. Copyright 1978 by Michael McClure. Reprinted by permission of New Directions Publishing Corp., 80 8th Ave., New York, NY 10011.

Untitled by Joho and *Untitled* by Dogen, both translated by Lucien Stryk and Takashi Ikemoto. From the book *Zen Poems of China and Japan* by Lucien Stryk and Takashi Ikemoto, pp. 15 and xlv. Copyright 1973 by Lucien Stryk, Takashi Ikemoto and Taigan Takayama. Reprinted by permission of Grove Press, 841 Broadway, New York, NY 10003.

Untitled by John Henry Newman is in the public domain.

Poems in Chapter 6

In by Vicente Huidobro, translated by H. R. Hays. From the book *12 Spanish American Poets* by H. R. Hays

(New Haven: Yale University Press, 1943), p. 79. Copyright 1971 by H. R. Hays. Reprinted by permission of Mrs. Juliette Hays.

The Heart of Secrets by Hilary Huttner. Copyright 1995 by Frontline Systems, Inc. Reprinted by permission of Frontline Systems, Inc., P.O. Box 4288, Incline Village 89450.

The Breathing and *City Psalm* by Denise Levertov. From the book *Poems 1960-1967* by Denise Levertov, pp. 80 and 222. Copyright 1966 by Denise Levertov. Reprinted by permission of New Directions Publishing Corp., 80 8th Ave., New York, NY 10011.

When you open your eyes deep in a wave by Karol Wojtyla, translated by Jerzy Peterkiewicz. From the book *Collected Poems: Karol Wojtyla* translated by Jerzy Peterkiewicz, p. 5. Copyright 1979, 1982 by Libreria Editrice Vaticana, Vatican City. Reprinted by permission of Random House, Inc., 201 E. 50th St., New York, NY 10022.

Untitled by Bunan, translated by Lucien Stryk and Takashi Ikemoto. From the book *Zen Poems of China and Japan* by Lucien Stryk and Takashi Ikemoto, p. 140. Copyright 1973 by Lucien Stryk, Takashi Ikemoto and Taigan Takayama. Reprinted by permission of Grove Press, 841 Broadway, New York, NY 10003.

I Built My Hut by T'ao Ch'ien, *Song of Myself, 50* by Walt Whitman, *God's Grandeur* by Gerard Manley Hopkins and *The Word* by Richard Realf are in the public domain.

Poems in Chapter 7

The Heart of Herakles by Kenneth Rexroth. From the book *Collected Shorter Poems* by Kenneth Rexroth. Copyright 1956 by Kenneth Rexroth. Reprinted by permission of New Directions Publishing Corp., 80 8th Ave., New York, NY 10011.

Renascence by Edna St. Vincent Millay. From the book *Collected Poems* by Edna St. Vincent Millay (New York: HarperCollins, 1971), pp. 3-13 passim. Copyright 1912, 1913, 1940, 1941 by Edna St. Vincent Millay. Now in the public domain.

Many Truly by Hugo Von Hofmannsthal, translated by Vernon Watkins. From the book *An Anthology of German Poetry* edited by Angel Flores (New York: Anchor Books, 1960), p. 332. Copyright 1960 by Vernon Watkins. Reprinted by permission of the estate of Vernon Watkins.

The Elusive Ones by Rumi, translated by John Moyne and Coleman Barks. From the book *Open Secret* by John Moyne and Coleman Barks, p. 30. Copyright 1984 by Threshold Books. Reprinted by permission of Threshold Books, RD 3, Box 208, Dusty Ridge Rd., Putney, VT 05346.

On the Beach at Night Alone by Walt Whitman, *Over All Presides the Universal Soul* by Plotinus, *All Are But Parts* by Alexander Pope, and *I Saw One Life and Felt that It Was Joy* by William Wordsworth are in the public domain.

Poems in Chapter 8

Vacillation, i by William Butler Yeats. From the book *Collected Poems* by William Butler Yeats (New York: Macmillan Company, 1940), p. 296. Copyright 1940 by W. B. Yeats. Reprinted by permission of Simon & Schuster, Inc., 1633 Broadway, New York, NY 10019.

Untitled by Uvavnuk. From the book *The Enlightened Heart* by Stephen Mitchell, p. 123. Copyright 1989 by Stephen Mitchell. Reprinted by permission of

He Walketh by Day translated by Robert Hillyer. From the book *An Anthology of World Poetry* edited by Mark Van Doren (New York: Harcourt, Brace & Company, 1936), p. 243. Copyright 1923 by B. J. Brimmer Company. Reprinted by permission of Francesca and Elizabeth Hillyer.

God's Harp by Gustav Falke, *The Prisoner* by Emily Brontë, *Heart of God* by Vachel Lindsay, and *Songs of Kabir*, II. 40 by Kabir are in the public domain.

INDEX OF TITLES

All Are But Parts 164
Alto Song 80
Below Freezing 74
Breathing, The 132
Chosen Site 44
City Psalm 136
Curative Powers of Silence, The 54
Dover Beach 72
Elusive Ones, The 174
Excerpt from Milarepa Tells His Story 84
Forgotten 202
Full Moon 108
Gitanjali (CIII) 62
God's Grandeur 142
God's Harp 194
God's World 192
Heart of God 208
Heart of Herakles, The 156
Heart of Secrets, The 130
He Walketh by Day 212
Holy Longing, The 36
How Sweet the Moonlight 76
I Built My Hut 125
I Saw One Life 176
I Thank You God for Most this Amazing 110
If Only There Were Stillness 60
In 128
Infinite, The 34
In Old Age 210
Latest Freed Man, The 104
Lines, Composed a Few Miles above Tintern Abbey 27
List, The 112
Many Truly 172

Now the Hour Bows Down 198
On the Beach at Night Alone 158
Over All Presides the Universal Soul 156
Prayer 58
Prisoner, The 204
Renascence 166
Shadows 100
Shores of Silence 64
Song, A 52
Song of Myself 134
Song of the Prophet to the San Juan River 56
Songs of Kabir 216
Stanzas Concerning an Ecstasy 38
Sweet Moment 200
Tea at the Palaz of Hoon 48
Untitled by Bunan 144
Untitled by Dogen 118
Untitled by Han-shan 86
Untitled by Jimenez 82
Untitled by Joho 116
Untitled by Newman 95
Untitled by Shutaku 196
Untitled by Uvavnuk 185
Vacillation 188
When I Am Not Dead 98
When You Open Your Eyes 138
Word, The 146
World Is Too Much with Us, The 74

INDEX OF AUTHORS

Arnold, Matthew 72
Beaumont, Joseph 56
Blake, William 5-6, 7
Brontë, Emily 204
Bunan 144
Ciardi, John 98
Coleridge, Samuel Taylor 14
Crashaw, Richard 52
cummings, e. e. 110
Dogen 118
Egyptian 212
Eliot, T. S. 8
Emerson, Ralph Waldo 8
Falke, Gustav 194
Ginsberg, Allen 11-12
Goethe, Johann Wolfgang von 36
Herbert, George 60
Halevi, Judah 210
Hall, Donald 14
Han-shan 88
Hofmannsthal, Hugo von 172
Hopkins, Gerard Manley 142
Huidobro, Vicente 128
Huttner, Hilary 80, 130, 200
Jiménez, Juan Ramón 82
Joho 114
Kabir 216
Keats, John 15
Lawrence, D. H. 7, 100
Levertov, Denise 132, 136
Leopardi, Giacomo 34
Lindsay, Vachel 208
Longfellow, Henry Wadsworth 14

McClure, Michael 112
Milarepa 84
Millay, Edna St. Vincent 166, 192
Navaho 54
Newman, John Henry 95
Paz, Octavio 202
Plotinus 160
Pope 164
Realf, Richard 146
Rexroth, Kenneth 156
Rilke, Rainer Maria 62, 198
Rumi 174
San Juan de la Cruz 38
Shakespeare, William 76
Shelley, Percy Bysshe 5, 10
Shutaku 196
Stevens, Wallace 48, 104
Tanikawa, Shuntaro 44
T'ao Ch'ien 125
Tranströmer, Tomas 74
Tu Fu, 108
Uvavnuk 185
Whitman, Walt 16, 134, 158
Wojtyla, Karol 64, 138
Wordsworth, William 27, 78, 176
Yeats, William Butler 188
Young, Al 58